she gets It!

The 11 Lies that
Hold Women Hostage

DRENDA KEESEE

DESTINY IMAGE® PUBLISHERS, INC.

P.O. Box 310, Shippensburg, PA 17257-0310

"Speaking to the Purposes of God for This Generation and for the Generations to Come."

This book and all other Destiny Image, Revival Press, MercyPlace, Fresh Bread, Destiny Image Fiction, and Treasure House books are available at Christian bookstores and distributors worldwide.

Previously published by Free Indeed Publishers copyright 2010.

For a U.S. bookstore nearest you, call 1-800-722-6774.

For more information on foreign distributors, call 717-532-3040.

Or reach us on the Internet: www.destinyimage.com.

Trade Paper ISBN 13: 978-0-7684-3698-3
Hardcover ISBN 13: 978-0-7684-3699-0
Large Print ISBN 13: 978-0-7684-3700-3
Ebook ISBN 13: 978-0-7684-9021-3

For Worldwide Distribution, Printed in the U.S.A.

1 2 3 4 5 6 7 / 15 14 13 12 11

To all the women who sincerely seek love and answers…
and to the people who have helped me find mine:

My loving, patient husband and best friend, Gary,
and our five amazing children:
Amy, Timothy, Thomas, Polly, and Kirsten;
you are my greatest reward.

My dearest mother and father, Polly and Don.

And Pastor Victor P. and Lois Rockhill,
whose faithfulness and labor in my life were not in vain.

ACKNOWLEDGMENTS

Special thanks to
the women at Faith Life Church,
XM Youth Ministry, and "the original team,"
Lance, my wonderful editor,
and all the people who have given their time,
mentorship, and friendship into my life,
teaching me the most valuable of life lessons.

ENDORSEMENTS

I can't think of a better title for Drenda Keesee's new book, because there's no question—this woman *gets it*. With her husband Gary, she's built a successful business, has an incredible family, and launched a global ministry helping people get out of debt and discover financial success. This isn't just a life story, it's a textbook for living life to the max. *She Gets It* and you need to get it, too.

In a world where the media focuses on shallow celebrity, *She Gets It* is the story of a woman of real depth. Drenda Keesee started with very little, and has become a serious force in the world. This is a significant model for what 21st century women can become.

Phil Cooke,
Filmmaker and Author of *Branding Faith*

Many of the pages of this book, I can relate to. I was so lost in being something for everyone else. I didn't know who I was. Charles and Frances Hunter's daughter, my girls' Mom, his wife, co-pastor of a church....where was Joan in all this. The freedom that I discovered in my mid-forty's was awesome. It gave me a whole now look on life and about me and who I was and who I AM. *She Gets It!* gives you a greater understanding of what has happened to so many people (male and female) and the journey to find the real you.

Joan Hunter
Author and Evangelist
President, Joan Hunter Ministries

A treasure trove of nuggets confirmed by Scripture and lived out in real testimony by a friend and a woman who because She Gets It----Got It! The 'How' book for women to find their position, personhood, purposed and prosperity in Christ.

Dr. Dean Radtke
Founder and CEO of Ministry Institute

This book is surprisingly interesting and surprisingly powerful! It paints a vivid display of God's desire for all of us to finally "get it". Thank you Drenda, for helping us "get it" even more!

Marty Copeland
Founder of Higher Fitness Ministries

If you're looking for a book that packs life-changing truth in a conversational, encouraging gift box you can count on Drenda to hold your hand and kick your (spriritual and emotional) derriere at the same time. It's quite rare to find the combination of truth-teller, confidante, and easy laugh in one person, but Drenda brings it, which is why she is beloved by so many, including me.

Anita Renfroe,
Comedian and Author

Drenda Keesee has written a great book about being a strong woman, which is both biblical and practical. She uses spiritual truths and personal experience to back her points. The book has a conversational tone, using a perfect blend of humor and seriousness to convey her message. Any woman should read this point if she wants a better understanding of how to "get IT!"

Pamela Lake
Brian Lake Ministries

CONTENTS

my search for "IT"

Created for Love and Commitment

Pursuing "IT"

my search for "IT"

One is not born,
but rather becomes,
a woman.

Simone de Beauvoir

I have spent most of my life searching for "IT."

Perhaps you have as well. If so, you know something of my personal quest and struggle to find the answer to the frightening question, "Who am I?" Unsure of who I was, I was left on my own to figure out how to live my life as a woman—to discover what would make me happy and how I could find true success as well as relationships that wouldn't disappoint me and leave me broken.

Not surprisingly, my search led me into the women's movement, with its promises of freedom to lead and plan my own life and control my destiny. Convinced that I could never trust men, I vowed to never allow a man to hurt me or to experience divorce, which I reasoned could be solved simply by just not getting married in the first place. Magazines, women's television programs, and self-help books told me "who" I was supposed to be, but their definition of womanhood was always changing just enough to keep me confused and yet chasing the elusive carrot and buying all their wares. They never told me "how" to truly be happy, and I never found out precisely what feminism is.

I lived through the "Whatever Feels Good, Just Do It" age, and I understand why so many of today's women are asking, "WHAT are we doing? WHO are we, anyway?" With so many different messages on womanhood being bantered around today, women are rightfully confused. What had once offered women security in life has been taken away, and women have been left to rummage through the remnants of past decades and movements in the hopes of finding some meaning to life.

After living this life for 40-plus years, I can finally say, "I GET IT!" And "IT" is not what most women think "IT" is.

Created for Love and Commitment

I wrote *She Gets It* to provide other women with answers that help them find their identity and value and show them how to make life choices that bring the real desire that every woman has—*to be loved and to love the woman she has become, through all the seasons and changes of life.* I have learned that most women's magazines, such as *Cosmopolitan,* don't know what "IT" is, and most female talk show hosts really don't have "IT" themselves, and they can't give away what they don't have. Rather, they can only offer women their flawed viewpoints of life—primarily how to be financially and professionally successful, divorced, or "playing the field" single—but the result of following their mantras is a large contingency of lonely women. Although they may make a difference for some, their personal anecdotes fail to deliver what every woman wants to experience at the deepest level of her being.

We are created for love and commitment, but most women are taught to be afraid of "IT" and think they can replace "IT" with one-night stands, paychecks and promotions, the latest sexual positions, and outdoing men before they undo them. And while I admire the philanthropy of some of Hollywood's hotties, I don't think their in-and-out-of relationships and short-lived marriages or orchestrated "new families," as Tyra Banks puts it, are what God had in mind to give women the joy of family, getting old with a man who comes to you and you go to exclusively for life. I am convinced that sex with my man of 27 years is better than the self-focused attempt of the age to buy endless boyfriends (or girlfriends) to meet our need for love. We live in a generation that seems to think it's impossible to have real love that lasts for a lifetime, and yet we are created at the core of our being to experience that kind of love.

> The greatest happiness of life is the conviction that we are loved—loved for ourselves, or rather, loved in spite of ourselves.
> VICTOR HUGO

Most women's organizations and conferences talk about the pain, the hurt, and the brokenness that evil men inflict upon us. Some also share how God loves us anyway, and we just need to trump life by becoming like the men who've hurt us in our pursuit to attain equality. Many seek to empower us by telling us it's all about us and how we need to take charge and never trust anyone but ourselves. "Make enough money and you can buy anything you want and do whatever you want." However, they fail to take into account the truth the Beatles sang so many years ago, "Money can't buy me love."

While I recognize the fact that we all have experienced pain, I want us to stop wallowing in the hurt of yesterday and start celebrating God's answers today so we can break free from the cycle of getting hurt again and again. So much of this pain is avoidable for us and our daughters if we understand how we got in this place to begin with, and if we truly understand how to live "IT" the right way and have the faith to carry "IT" out until we see change and results. We can't run from "IT" or make enough money to escape our need for relationships that have commitment, fulfillment, and selfless giving. How we live is important after all.

Pursuing "IT"

My personal journey led me to some of the same conclusions that most of the women in our age have drawn. For instance, "You can't trust men, so use them before they use you" was once my personal motto, but something drastic altered that picture for me and changed my life forever. I discovered "IT" as a result and have spent my entire life pursuing a deeper understanding of "IT." After seeing it all come full circle, I know that "IT" really works. I am now enjoying the choice to live "IT" every day of my life. I couldn't be happier or more fulfilled.

As a college student, early one morning I had a dream that is as vivid in my mind today as it was back then. I was lying on a dirty floor in a windowless room and surrounded by many women who were missing body parts—some their arms, others legs, and some were even missing from their torso down. We were locked in an old house that was filled with the constant moans and groans of hurting women. The agony was intense, and the darkness very grave. All I heard were sighs, moans, and deep sobbing—no one spoke words.

There were so many sobs reverberating in the house that I could hear nothing else. It was horrific, and I desperately wanted to get up and do something about it, but I was missing my legs from the knees down and couldn't do anything. I began to cry out to God for deliverance from the misery. As I did, I surrendered myself to God and began to worship Him. I tried to sit up to praise Him. It was a struggle, but as I did, my legs began to grow out, and I became whole again. Thrilled, I rose to my feet and began to try to lift others. The women around me began to heal as well and rise up. As one woman after another lifted the women next to them, we all became whole and stood together rejoicing. The darkness was replaced with a great light, and the sorrow was turned into dancing.

I was awakened from this amazingly vivid dream by the ring of my dormitory phone. I picked up the phone, and it was a boyfriend with whom I had tried to end our relationship several times, but he kept calling to get me to come back to him. As he spoke, I heard another voice on the inside of me say, "You were running a good race. Who cut in to keep you from your prize?" I suddenly knew this was God speaking to me, and the message couldn't have been clearer: This relationship was a counterfeit, and my old boyfriend was attempting to steer me away from the destiny God had for me and from becoming whole.

> ...to bestow on them a crown of beauty instead of ashes, the oil of gladness instead of mourning, and a garment of praise instead of a spirit of despair (ISAIAH 61:3).

At the time, I was incredibly insecure and afraid. What if I let go of this relationship? Would there be anyone or anything else for me? Yet the dream was so strong—so real to me. So I ended the relationship and said, "God, whatever You have for my life, that's what I want to live."

The journey begins....

get Lost:

HOW DID WE GET IN THIS MESS?

1

get Lost:

HOW DID WE GET IN THIS MESS?

> The world is...a kind of spiritual kindergarten
> where millions of bewildered infants are trying
> to spell "God" with the wrong blocks.
>
> **Edwin Arlington Robinson**

I can't help but think that my story has been repeated over and over in different times and cultural settings throughout history. Times change, but women and our problems in the search for love do not. Women are, by nature, before being hardened by the world's ills, willing and desirous to help others—to give and receive love. In every woman lies a deep yearning to be understood, to be loved, to be told how important she is, and touched in her heart and body. Yet throughout history, we have a track record of falling into traps, abusive relationships, and following men—and women—who have promised us love, answers, success, and whatever else we've sought after, with bad results. It's not always men who mess up women's lives! Many a woman has destroyed a man's life as well. It's a crazy cycle of "I'll get you before you get me" that no one ultimately wins.

Losing Our Way

Somehow, someway, both men and women have lost their way. I don't think there has ever been a time in history when more people have lost their way. We have more information and more promises of every possible cure for what ails us in countless books, blogs, magazines, television programs, pills, and "you name it," and yet we seem to still be lost.

My husband teases that his GPS's name is Drenda. I am his constant companion and the hope that he won't end up lost somewhere. Even so, we've made an occasional wrong turn and gotten lost for a while. But I'm not talking about having a destination and making a simple wrong turn. I'm talking about the kind of lost where we don't even know "where" the destination is, much less know how to get there. We humans have lost our way and have no idea where to find it.

Like the time my mother and I were returning to Georgia from a funeral in Alabama. We started in the right direction, but in the midst of conversation, we somehow got on the expressway headed west. *Hours* went by. To our shock, we crossed the Mississippi state line before we realized we had headed in the totally wrong direction. Exhausted and tired, we stopped at a Cracker Barrel, had dinner, then got back on the expressway and headed east. It was late, and we were extremely tired. How much time had we wasted going in a direction that took us farther and farther from our destination? We had missed our purpose.

> Thus does the world forget You, its Creator, and falls in love with what You created instead of with You.
>
> AUGUSTINE

Our travel fiasco mirrors so many people's lives. Looking for happiness and love, many of us pursued it in the wrong direction, which we didn't know was the wrong way until we ended in a place that was nothing like the destination we sought to achieve. Realizing we were lost, we looked for answers from female icons of our day, but all we received was a lot of superfluous talk, more about feeding our needs through a stopover on the road than heading in the right direction to begin with and truly enjoying the rewards of the journey.

We're lost all right, but we don't know it oftentimes until it's almost too late and we're too tired to fix it. Then someone comes up with a new stopover, such as "If you're not enjoying love and sex at home, an extramarital affair will surely fix it." "You deserve to be loved." "Have it your way." "Use him before he uses you." "Twelve new sexy makeup techniques." "Leave your man for a female partner." A lot of talk; most of which is bad advice, and it's certainly not the destination. We are still lost.

Is there a way home?

Understand Your Purpose

To know my destination in life, I first need to understand my purpose. If I want to fix something that is broken, I have to go back to the original design to discover how it was intended to function. Whether you believe there is a Designer or not, it's hard to deny the intricate, amazing details of our bodies, the earth, the animals, vegetation, weather patterns, galaxies, and the unique imprint of every human being—not to mention the different complementary design of men and women. *There is a Designer of our lives and world, so there is a plan and purpose and function for our lives.*

As I've read and studied Genesis 3, I've come to understand the "earth curse" that came upon all of creation at The Fall of man and woman in the Garden of Eden and the staggering impact of that curse. I think most of the answers to life's questions lie in the dawn of creation. That curse affects every area of our lives, from our outlook on life to our finances to our relationships. The curse reads, "*Cursed is the ground because of you; through painful toil you will eat of it all the days of your life. It will produce thorns and thistles for you*" (Gen. 3:17–18). This was spoken to Adam because of his act of disobedience against God. God said, "Because of you" these things happened.

It was never God's intention for us to live in a world filled with so much pain and suffering. Everything He made was good, and the earth was given to man and to woman as a great gift to enjoy. Some people argue about why a loving God would let them make the decision to obey or disobey His rule, but the fact is that without choices, love is not love. God did not force the objects of His love—the man and woman—to follow Him or serve His plan for their lives. Love isn't love if you have to force someone to give it to you or coerce them to share their life with you. Even if you buy it with favors, money, or anything else, it's bribery, not true love.

As a result of The Fall, Adam had a strong diversion from not only his love for God that day, but also from the incredible woman who had been given to him as an amazing gift to love and cherish. Before his treasonous act, he was able to focus on loving his wife and sharing with her in the pleasures of the Garden and its beauty. Now he had to focus on trying to fight against thorns and thistles and the earth curse to make it through just another day. *Survival became his way of life, and loving Eve fell by the wayside.* A man's strong sex drive and need to have a physical release would drive him back to his wife at times, but his focus became how to scratch out a living, how to survive. Pressure and pain replaced the provision that God originally gave him in the Garden of abundant delight.

Sharing in the Earth Curse

In the biblical account of The Fall, I want to focus on what happened to not only Eve, but to every daughter of Eve who would draw a breath after her. Besides sharing in the earth curse that would require her and her husband to look for provision and fight to eek out a living, another curse came upon her and all womankind. She was instructed that because she was deceived and misused her influence on her husband, she would have *pain in childbirth, a longing desire for her husband and his attention (which would go unfulfilled), and her husband would rule over her* (see Gen. 3:16).

Instead of Adam loving her the way he was originally intended, his focus would be consumed by conquering contenders, and that would keep him occupied and busy, too busy for his wife. She would spend her time trying to get his love and attention, and it would fall continually short of her desire. Not to mention, he would often see her as a contender as well. She would make demands on him for love and become critical when he wasn't "there" for her. Emotional outbursts and disrespectful words would replace her love and respect for him. The man and woman would be caught in a tug of war to get what they "needed" instead of lovingly providing for each other's needs. He would resort to harsh rule over her instead of treating her as the companion and friend who was taken from his side and created to be a helper and lover in his life.

> The mass of men [and women] live lives of quiet desperation.
> **HENRY THOREAU**

What a mess everything became. From this point forward, turmoil entered all relationships, especially between men and women. When Adam and Eve messed up things in the Garden, they hid from God in fear (see Gen. 3:8). Insecurity and guilt ruled their lives, and *every person born into the earth-cursed system has experienced the same loss of completeness.* God called out to them in their hiding, and they responded that they were hiding because they were "naked and ashamed." Before this, the Book of Genesis records that when God made them, "they were naked and not ashamed." They had no secrets, no fears, and no abusive attitudes toward each other. They had real love and real companionship, where they were happily working together and sharing a deep love.

Yet when God finds them, Adam says, "The woman *you* put here with me—she gave me some fruit from the tree, and I ate it" (see Gen. 3:12, emphasis mine). Not only did he blame his wife, Adam blamed God as well! After his accusation of the woman, God turned to her and asked her what she had done. I think He asked her in a tender way. She explained that her actions were due to the serpent's lying deception, which had come through the promise of being made wise like God if she would eat the fruit. God was not in any way caught off guard by her misunderstanding and emotionally based bad decision. Satan, the enemy of God who had been rejected for high treason and rebellion (see Isa. 14:12–15), had instructed Adam and Eve how to follow the same path. *The curse they received was brought on by their own actions; it was not God's desire or decision to curse them.* He had given them a choice to love Him, and they had decided to go their own way. The Scripture reads, "*Cursed is the ground because of you*"—pain in life had come.

The insecurity they both felt alienated them in their relationship as well. Fears of how to navigate through life, and the pain of being separated from the love they had known, surely left them blaming each other. Adam blamed Eve for the calamity and went so far as to try to shift the blame to God. There must have been a tremendous amount of brokenness in their home, because their children, Cain and Abel, the very first children on earth, got into strife and Cain murdered Abel (see Gen. 4:8). Children learn from their parents, and the idea to abuse or even murder another human being must have been modeled in the displays of anger they witnessed in their parents' lives.

As It Was in the Beginning

Women and men today suffer the same deceptions, misunderstandings, and out-of-whack priorities originating from this earth-cursed system. When you understand the effects of The Fall of humankind, you can see and begin to understand the vain endeavor of both men and women to regain their identity in the wrong ways. It is not surprising that men often seek to get their sole identity from their careers and successes, trying to conquer the earth curse through hard work and long hours, neglecting their spouses and children. Their wives complain of their lack of involvement in the family, and strife results as the two of them fight each other trying to get their needs met in the relationship. Children often become the bargaining chip and the real losers of the game.

Many men have resorted to simply pursuing their careers and having sex on the side, without a commitment to marriage. In their "success and money pursuit," they work and pursue sex wherever they see opportunities and have no time or interest to invest in long-term relationships. They have plenty of discretionary income to spend on themselves, vacations, the gym, and golf, because they have no children to support and no wives to take a cut.

And we did—or should I say, the women's movement,—did this to ourselves. Women have confided in me that they are now supporting their deadbeat husband because he never worked, and now that they are divorced she has to pay him alimony! She pursued a career to take care of her family, and now he gets a large part of it. Is this the equality we thought would free us from the pains of the earth-cursed system? The deliverance has taken on many names, but *none have delivered women the true equality or love we have sought.*

> There is a God-shaped vacuum in every heart.
> BLAISE PASCAL

I can't tell you how many women I've talked to who are trying to pressure their "boyfriend" to make a decision to "get married" as they continue to live with him and give him the sexual benefits of a marriage commitment without any commitment. I always ask the women, "What reason does he have to make a commitment if everything he's looking for is given to him without one?" When these men finally concede to the pressure to prove their love through a wedding and do get married, these relationships seldom last a year. Then they are both on the prowl again, looking for another fix for his sexual needs and new reassurances in her quest for love. Their insecurities only increase through the brokenness of the relationship, and the reaffirmation that men and women can't get along with each other is heightened.

How many billions of dollars do women spend annually trying to figure out how to get men's love and devotion? Fads, makeup, fashion, and diet pills are all a part of the chase. Check the headlines in the tabloids at the grocery checkout counter: "How to Get Your Man to Notice You" and "Sex Secrets That Will Keep Him Coming Back." All of these vain promises have turned any hope of lasting and meaningful relationships into mere hype.

One of the frightening outcomes of a self-focused pursuit to get love is the tragic headline of a mother who allows her own child to be abused in order to "keep" a man. I can think of no greater fall of humankind than the protective and nurturing desire of a mother perverted against her own daughter for personal gain. Then there is also the message of abortion, the same brand of destroying a child in order to pursue "self." The insecurity of The Fall is just reenacted over and over in her life as her choices mimic those of her ancestors, and her choices produce the same death and destruction that Adam and Eve witnessed in their lives and in their children.

A woman who discovers "IT" can never be happy destroying others to get what she wants.

Searching for a Fix

Everywhere I turn, I see the breakdown of this earth-cursed system in the lives of women, men, children, and society as a whole. We seem to run from one person's opinion to another's on "how to fix it." We change our theories about life, love, happiness, and relationships, but we don't find the answers; otherwise, the merchandising of "answers" would have halted long ago.

Untold sums of money are made selling women "the look" and telling them how to achieve it. I am not against fashion or looking wonderful, but I see so much focus on outward beauty and so many selfish attitudes that go with the pursuit of self that any external vision of beauty is lost. My mother said it best (probably on our extended road trip to Mississippi), "Pretty is as pretty does." We don't act so pretty because something on the inside is wrong. *It seems easier to focus on what we see in the mirror rather than on "who" we are and what makes us beautiful on the inside and the outside.*

Young women are the most vulnerable. Older women are driving the car in the wrong direction, and young women are following on a quicker path of destruction. The desire to get a man to love them has translated into women hooking up, having sex on the first date, and spending untold amounts of money, time, and energy trying to compete with other women for the "man" of her dreams.

Women spend a large amount of their time in front of the mirror, trying to decide if they look beautiful, sexy, and desirable. They ask questions about their looks and seek approval for just about everything on a constant basis. Most women wake up every day looking for outside stimulus from compliments, a second look from an adoring man, or the affirmation that the mirror tells them they match the latest view of beauty as seen in the images of magazines and movies.

> A voice in the wind
> I do not know;
> A meaning on the face
> of the high hills
> Whose utterance
> I cannot comprehend.
> A something is
> behind them:
> that is God.
> GEORGE MACDONALD

The way a woman packages herself has a lot to say about her and will attract that kind of person. If she dresses sensually, more than likely she will attract a man who is interested in her for her sensuality. If a woman wants to attract a man who respects her as a woman of God, she should reflect that in the way she carries herself and dresses. The outside should reflect the inside with beauty, modesty, and sincerity.

"Your desire [longing] will be for your husband, and he will rule over you." *It sounds like the earth curse is still working.*

More and more women are throwing off the "man thing," and some have resorted to female partners who really "get them." Or they've resorted to self-made fantasies such as I noticed in the December 2009 *Glamour* magazine: "Nothing's more invigorating than sex. Have sex with yourself on your lunch hour." I can think of nothing emptier than that.

How lost have we become?

Instead of going back to the original Designer and fixing it according to His design, we say, "Why not just throw out the design and make something new, even if it still lacks? Men don't need women, either. We can have meaningful relationships and satisfy our appetite for sex with the same sex." Although this is not the first century in which people have drawn this conclusion, it's never become a workable long-term solution. Very, very few of these relationships are long term or successful, and it brings with it an entire new set of social problems, from who gets the surrogate child at separation to serious emotional, spiritual, and medical repercussions. Something's very wrong with this picture, and it completely misses the Designer's mark. It's a stopover but not even close to the real deal.

All in a Pursuit of Love

To keep from being lost or to help us find our way out of being lost, today's guides are the women's talk show hosts who try to tell us how to get to our destination—of how to get so-called love. We know love and security must be out there somewhere. We just don't know how to find it. We cry out for someone to please tell us how to get there, but all they tell us is "what to be." Nobody tells us "who we really are" or "what our purpose is and how to get there."

I came to a point where all my media mentors, my female icons, fell one at a time from the throne of popularity in my world. Many of the women who supposedly had "IT" died of overdoses, car wrecks, or murder; or suffered from alcoholism, career declines, divorces, or rumors of their selfish outbursts. It made me rethink the answers they had offered at the pinnacle of their popularity. I began to see them as puppets who had been used to sell a product or ideology while they were in the limelight. I even empathized and pitied some of them, because as a woman I could identify with the compromises they made to get what they thought would make them happy—only to end up disillusioned and with their hopes shattered in the process.

All in a pursuit of love.

Maybe that's why we're lost.

Do we even know what "love" is?

get Religion:
I DON'T THINK SO

The Good Girl/Bad Girl Syndrome

Religious Ladies

Where Is the Love?

God's Love Is Real

2
get Religion:
I DON'T THINK SO

If I were personally to define religion,
I would say that it is a bandage that
man has invented to protect a soul
made bloody by circumstances.

Theodore Dreiser

What is love, and how does one find it? If the world of fashionistas and the Hollywood crowd do not have the answer to finding "IT," then perhaps you think that religion has "IT."

I don't think so. Religion, which I define as an organized system of teaching with an approved pattern of behavior and a form of worship of God, has fallen short of giving us the answers as well. I grew up trying to be so good, to always do what was right, and to live up to a high moral standard. I was quick to find fault with those around me who made wrong decisions and didn't live up to the expectations I'd had placed upon me. I had lofty ambitions, but the harder I worked to achieve God's approval and others' approval through my own accomplishments, the less my accomplishment fulfilled me. Religion, or trying to do "right" by my own strength and working for love and approval, left me tired and frustrated and extraordinarily unfulfilled.

One day I woke up and decided that if being religious didn't make me happy or bring me love and acceptance, maybe the opposite would. I gave up trying to be "good" and sought pleasure and fun. I had tried the lifestyle of the "good girl" and found it did not satisfy, so I tried being the "bad girl," but it didn't take long to discover that did not answer my inner longings either. All that brought was guilt and shame followed by short-lived attempts to going back to being "good" again.

My religious attempts to find love and meaning only led me through a frustrating cycle from "good girl" to "bad girl," and both gave me lower self-esteem and brought me into deeper emptiness.

The Good Girl/Bad Girl Syndrome

Try hard to be good.
  Fail to achieve.
    Feel guilty.
      Give up.
    Be bad.
  Feel guilty.
Recommit.
Try hard again to be good.

If you've been both the "good girl" and the "bad girl," you know both involve the same root problem—both want love and acceptance; they just go about their pursuit in opposite ways. Both girls want to achieve love, and they are willing to work to be worthy of it. They are simply taking their cues from two very different sources.

The "good girl" takes her cue from the right and wrong of religion, and the constraints and the standards of religion give her a mark to try to work to accomplish. She has been given a standard to measure her life by and is left to achieve it by her own efforts and the sheer force of her will. She may find some comfort in the confines of the "dos and don'ts" and doesn't have to think too much, because most of the decisions regarding right and wrong have already been codified for her. Unfortunately, I found that almost everything enjoyable in life seemed to be listed as wrong within my religious background.

> Religion that is merely ritual and ceremonial can never satisfy. Neither can we be satisfied by a religion that is merely humanitarian or serviceable to mankind. Man's craving is for the spiritual.
>
> SAMUEL SHOEMAKER

For instance, in early church history, the church actually named the act of sex as the first sin. Saint Augustine (354–430), whose writings have had a profound effect on the church's theology, believed that the original sin of Adam and Eve introduced a fundamental disorder into human sexual desire. The equating of sin with sex is evident throughout Augustine's writing. Not surprisingly, this flawed concept has tainted the beauty and pleasure of sex within marriage. Women in early British history were told to picture making an army for the queen during sex just to get through it. It is no wonder that so many women have left religion over this distorted view of sexuality and adopted other flawed perspectives on it that are equally or even more hurtful.

Religion recognizes the problems of society and tries to achieve the answer. Eventually, religion itself becomes a counterfeit lover for real intimacy. I have a good friend who says the word *intimacy* means "in-to-me-see." No matter how pure my desire is to do what is right, if I mask my inadequacy and insecurities with religion, I am left with my human effort that is always going to lack. Within religion, I don't find the love I am looking for; I just make conditions for love to exist, but I can't live up to them. So then I have no intimacy in my life, just an emotional affair with intimacy. I have covered myself and hidden behind religion, but the real me, with all my suppressed appetites, remains unfulfilled.

It goes back to the earth curse I wrote about in the previous chapter. I still have deep longings. I still want love. I just suppress it. My standard is a hard taskmaster, and when my performance falls short, I am stripped of my dignity and self-worth. I am constantly reminded that I am a failure and that my ability, looks, or whatever it is I am trying to achieve always falls short of the perfect, the ideal. I can never do it "good enough" or be "good enough" to reach perfection. As I keep striving and failing to reach the mark, the only recourse I have is to find faults in my fellow females and point out their shortcomings; and by comparing myself to them, I look and feel so much better. That's why religious or "good girls" take pride in judging "bad girls," and "bad girls" who have been converted over to religion make the best "judges." They have a lot more to cover.

I hear all the "bad girls" saying, "Yeah! Tell it like it is. What a bunch of hypocrites the religious girls are! And they say we are bad!"

But wait just a minute. We are all in the same state of error. The "bad girl" does the same thing as the "good girl" except that her value is based on a whole different code of ethics. She has been disappointed and hurt enough that she knows she can't trust anyone else, so she must look out for herself. She rebelled against the idea of trying to be perfect, and since she knows it isn't attainable, she feels it makes much more sense to just let loose and have fun and to get hers before she is gotten by someone else.

The "bad girl" settles for what feels good to her now, with no or little thought of the consequences. She doesn't just have a mental or emotional affair, as the "good girl" does—she has the actual affair! Her pain seeks to find pleasure in the moment. She doesn't mind being seductive, blatantly sexy, and promiscuous. She learns to work the system and freely offers what she has to get love (and sometimes favors or money). She figures the way to get love is to use her charms to her advantage and disregard the fearful religious judgments. She is ready to be in the spotlight, at least for a season. She hardens herself and tells herself she's going to be fine. No one is using her any more than she is using them.

As a young woman, when I demanded my own way, my mother always told me, "Drenda, selfishness produces loneliness." When we go after what we want and don't care who gets hurt or how we go about getting it, our demands are in vain. We may get what we desire for a season, but it will turn back on us and bury us in a sea of loneliness. In the earlier years, I swam around, thrashing my arms about and grabbing what I wanted, but after a while, I was swimming alone.

> Religion is man's quest for God; the Gospel is the Savior God seeking lost men. Religion is man-made; the Gospel is the gift of God. Religion is the story of what a sinful man tries to do for a holy God; the Gospel is the story of what a holy God has done for sinful men. Religion is good views; the Gospel is good news.
>
> RON GUSTAFSON

It's a terrible place to be in, because of all the lies we have to tell ourselves to pretend that we are OK. In Isaiah 5:18–20, *The Message* Bible states it this way:

> *Doom to you who use lies to sell evil, who haul sin to market by the truckload. Who say, "What is God waiting for? Let Him get a move on so we can see it...." Doom to you who call evil good and good evil, who put darkness in place*

*of light and light in place of darkness, who substitute bitter
for sweet and sweet for bitter!*

Religious Ladies

In my pursuit to find meaning, answers, and love, I have been
both the "good girl" and the "bad girl." You have probably tried
it as well. Most of us have played on both sides of the street, if
we were given the option.

Take a look at the churchwomen of Zion who wanted it both
ways. In Isaiah 3:16–24, the women of Zion, whom we might
call the "religious ladies," decided to go after the cultural messages to the women of the land. They are characterized in *The
Message* in this way:

> God says, *"Zion women are stuck-up,*
> *prancing around in their high heels,*
> *Making eyes at all the men in the street,*
> *swinging their hips,*
> *Tossing their hair,*
> *gaudy and garish in cheap jewelry."*
>
> *The Master will fix it so those Zion women*
> *will all turn bald—*
> *Scabby, bald-headed women.*
> *The Master will do it.*

I see this as a picture of "exposure." In the culture of the day,
a woman's hair was considered a mark of her femininity, her
beauty, something that separated her from the boys. Baldness
was therefore a major curse and an exposé of what was beneath
the finery, revealing her real heart and attitude.

The time is coming when the Master will strip them of their fancy baubles—the dangling earrings, anklets and bracelets, combs and mirrors and silk scarves, diamond brooches and pearl necklaces, the rings on their fingers and the rings on their toes, the latest fashions in hats, exotic perfumes and aphrodisiacs, gowns and capes, all the world's finest in fabrics and design.

Instead of wearing seductive scents,
these women are going to smell like rotting cabbages;
Instead of modeling flowing gowns,
They'll be sporting rags;
Instead of their stylish hairdos,
scruffy heads;
Instead of beauty marks,
scabs and scars.

The *New International Version* states, "Instead of beauty, branding." It was as though they would be branded like cattle by the culture.

Isaiah goes on to say in chapter 4, verse 1,

That will be the day when seven women will gang up on one man, saying, "We'll take care of ourselves,
get our own food and clothes.
Just give us a child. Make us pregnant
so we'll have something to live for!"

We can see the disparity and hypocrisy of the "religious ladies." When they reach the end of their religious striving, they decide to follow the pattern of the women whom they see having what appears to be success with the men. They compromise, stick their nose in the air, and go after what they want in the name of self-preservation. No longer are they attempting to even live respectably. They offer the men anything they want just to get what they want. Seven women fighting after the same man and offering to pay their own way—no wedding, no commitment, just a sexual fling and a baby, hopefully, to fill the loneliness of their empty hearts.

> The world is perishing for lack of the knowledge of God, and the church is famishing for want of His Presence. The instant cure of most of our religious ills would be to enter the Presence in spiritual experience, to become suddenly aware that we are in God and that God is in us. This would lift us out of our pitiful narrowness and cause our hearts to be enlarged.
>
> A. W. TOZER

"Bad girls" and "good girls" do it. The tabloids and the church world, from the leadership down, are full of this kind of attitude. Many of these women were raised in church, and their grandmothers and mothers and aunts were "church ladies." Somewhere compromise came in, and they decided to pursue love through an "anything goes" attitude toward life. They talk of "spirituality," but there is no right or wrong anymore. The leftovers of religion have left a bad taste in their mouth, and it's easier to "have a form of godliness, but deny that there is any real power in truth."

I love what Isaiah 4:4 (MSG) says in answer to this broken picture of womanhood.

> God will give Zion's women a good bath. He'll scrub the bloodstained city of its violence and brutality, purge the place with a firestorm of judgment.

There has to be a stripping away of what is wrong in order to find that which is truly sacred. There is nothing like a good hot cleansing bath to take away the filth, the smut of living life without love. Underneath all that dirt there is potential, there is hope, there is the possibility for relationship, for true intimacy. This is how God describes it in the verses that follow in Isaiah:

> *Then God will bring back the ancient pillar of cloud by day and the pillar of fire by night and mark Mount Zion and everyone in it with His glorious presence, His immense, protective presence, shade from the burning sun and shelter from the driving rain.* (Isaiah 4:5 MSG)

"Then God." Two very powerful words. Religion attempts to get to God through works, but when our works fall short, *"Then God."* God figures a way to get to us and give us a bath.

Where Is the Love?

So where is the love we search for? It isn't in the glamour world. It's not in the religious world. Perhaps you wonder if it even exists.

The only woman who really knows love is the one who has experienced it firsthand and now "GETS IT" enough to share it with someone else. Her search for "IT" has to come to a place of receiving first, because she can't give it if she's never experienced "IT."

God Himself chose to intervene and give the women of Zion a bath, when they came to the realization of just how incapable they were of doing it for themselves. The "good girls" and the "bad girls" couldn't fix themselves with their counterfeit affections, their lovers, and their haughty judgmental airs. Neither education, career success, popularity, possessions, position, power over or praise of men and women, beauty, clothes, love of men or women, nor the greatest philanthropic endeavor in the world could wash away the stains. Now that they were bald, barren, and without love, they could see this.

> There is no need to plead that the love of God shall fill our heart as though He were unwilling to fill us. He is willing as light is willing to flood a room that is opened to its brightness; willing as water is willing to flow into an emptied channel. Love is pressing round us on all sides like air. Cease to resist, and instantly love takes possession.
>
> AMY CARMICHAEL

For the woman of Zion, only the real love of someone or something that was greater than the stench of her mistakes, bad decisions, and selfishness could do it. If He was dirty Himself, He would have no power to make her clean. He had to be spotless Himself to be able to love her in the way He did. To stoop to her level to give her a bath, that was real love. He gathered her in his arms. She was ashamed, lonely, almost despondent from a lack of love, from criticism, from her own fears and judgments and those of others. He didn't notice, or He chose not to notice. She gave herself willingly to Him, and He took her for His bride, committing to keep her safe and protecting her heart from the cold cruelties of the cursed world. His love made her radiant, and He began to teach her a new law, not the law of religion or the law of the streetwise, but rather the law of love that would never leave her or forsake her.

God's Love Is Real

I was lost. I was tired of all the "good girl" pursuits, the arrogance, and performance with passing accolades that left me weary and unfulfilled. I was guilty and ashamed of my "bad girl" days, and I was too tired of trying to figure out my life myself to keep going.

I had seen vague glimpses of a life I wanted in some of the "church ladies" I had come into contact with in the past, but even their lives were not always perfect or complete. Nevertheless, those past dim glimpses caused me to seek for security and to hide from my past within the walls of a church building under the direction of a loving pastor and joyous sound of a choir that attracted me. But it wasn't the trimmings of the church or its programs that caused me to return. I found something far deeper than that there.

While I could never explain precisely what I found there, my best description of it was some sort of liquid love. I felt it, sensed it, and knew something was different. I couldn't remember ever feeling so completely saturated with love. It was much more than the people who gathered there; in fact, they were about the most unlikely group of people to be mixed together in a stew of humanity. They were old, young, black, white, oriental, poor, rich, and from all classes. They hugged me, offered to pray for me, and even scared me with their bold demonstrations that seemed a bit strange at the time.

Beyond the church people, though, there was something else— or Someone else. I felt as though they were just the décor on the front door, leading into the real home for which I was searching. I gingerly tiptoed to that door and felt this overwhelming draw to go farther inside. It was as if all of the logical resistance I could muster, all the feminist jargon about how I didn't need anyone else but me, couldn't stop me from the irresistible love that was wooing me through the door. I tried to excuse the love that drew me ever closer. For a moment, I thought, *This is a trick, some kind of drug piped into the room to make me feel such an exuberant joy...like chocolate or shopping.*

But, no, I knew this was greater, much greater.

I began to weep uncontrollably as I discovered *love was real.* It was more than I deserved and greater than I could earn. It was not a feeling. It was not an earthly experience. It was a Person. His name was Jesus, and He had come to wash me...to draw me a bath and to cleanse me from my sin. I felt naked and ashamed in the presence of such love, but once He washed me, my sins that were like scarlet were made as white as new fallen snow (see Isa. 1:18). His love was pure, and He had given His life for me. He was the only One who could. He was perfect; He was love.

I was a young woman when I walked through the doors of the church where I found the love I had been looking for. I found "IT"—not in a pastor, a choir, or a teaching, but in Jesus Christ. To receive His love and life into the depths of my being was and remains the greatest intimacy I have ever experienced. To be fully known and yet deeply loved made me the happiest person on the planet and drew worship from the depths of my being. To not have to perform for His love, but just to receive Him, made me complete. I stopped searching for love and started giving it. I couldn't exhaust it. It never left. It's still working in me today. It changed everything.

I "GET IT."

get Freedom:

LIFE IN GOD'S KINGDOM

3

get Freedom:

LIFE IN GOD'S KINGDOM

Christ has set us free to live a free life.
So take your stand! Never again let anyone
put a harness of slavery on you.

Galatians 5:1 *The Message*

I like to pride myself on being adventurous—ready for anything and everything—and I have discovered that to live by faith is life's greatest adventure. To have my life in Jesus' hands and to follow Him has been a great comfort but also as unpredictable as a roller coaster. There have been ups and downs, but I know I am strapped in, committed to the journey, and I will arrive safely (and have fun). I have been on this amazing journey now for almost 30 years, and it just gets better and better. It has taken me far beyond anything I ever imagined.

To begin to walk by faith with God in His Kingdom is a totally different experience from trying to live by a religious standard. The day God washed me from my sin, and we exchanged our love in pledge, I gave Him everything, and He gave me everything. I found I had a new hunger to know and love God. I began to read the Bible and talk to God constantly, and my life and beliefs began to change radically as I learned from Him the way He does things. I was caught in the throes of His passion—He was my Lover, my Friend, and my constant Companion.

The apostle Paul said, *"If anyone is in Christ, he is a new creation; the old has gone, the new has come!"* (2 Cor. 5:17). In my life, many new things came, and many old things just passed away. Some went away without my notice, and with others I struggled to hold on to them until finally I could resist no longer, and I let go. Always for my best. Always for my good.

Living by God's standards brings great rewards. Today I am living a dream. Everything I really ever dreamed of becoming as a little girl—a schoolteacher, a television anchor, a counselor, a public speaker, a world traveler—I have been privileged to enjoy, but with God's special twist to make it a great surprise! I've even enjoyed some exciting adventures beyond my wildest dreams.

Kingdom Life

One of the areas of my life that I struggled to give God was my complete dependence on Him. Actually, I think a better word would be *trust*. It's not that I didn't find Him completely trustworthy; it's just that I wanted to maintain control until I was sure. The principles for living in His Kingdom are completely based on faith in Him and His Word and promises, and I found I had to let go in order to receive. *"Give, and it will be given to you"* is one of the most basic teachings of Jesus (Luke 6:38), which is the opposite of what you and I learned in the earth-cursed system. The earth curse says, "Hold on to your life. Fight for it. Don't trust anyone with it. Look out for number one. Take but don't give." I had tried that, and the results were loneliness and brokenness.

Now, Jesus was telling me to give it all away—not so much money or possessions, although I would learn to trust Him with those as well. This was more difficult to do—it was my entire life He wanted. My allegiance. My destiny. My love. I knew He promised, "*Never will I leave you; never will I forsake you*" (Heb. 13:5), but I was afraid of what would happen if I was not able to stay committed to my part of the agreement. I found out that getting washed alone didn't always keep me from getting dirty again. What then? What if I failed Him? Would He still love me? I was afraid to let go, because if I did, and then I failed, how miserable would the failure be? How low would I sink if I had finally found love and then lost it?

> Our only business is to love and delight ourselves in God.
> BROTHER LAWRENCE

I set out feverishly to learn all I could about the new Kingdom He brought me into and the obedience it required, so I wouldn't get booted out into the cold darkness (my perception, not His character). Even though He promised to never send me away, I still had to grow in my faith in Him and His promises to experience true freedom. I was watching over my shoulder for constant reassurances that He was still there. When I would slip, disobey, or dishonor Him with my actions, He was still there, waiting for me to come back home. Even when I wasn't faithful to Him, He was always faithful to me (see 2 Tim. 2:13).

I had received forgiveness for my past and redemption from the earth curse. I just didn't know the Kingdom and His love in a deep enough way to truly experience the freedom that was already given to me. Jesus took me beyond my pensive walk into a love journey, learning new ways He would show me His love every day for eternity. What a deep love!

Over time, my confidence in Christ grew, and for the first time in my life, I felt free, really free! With this freedom came the inner strength to challenge wrong attitudes, fears, and selfishness.

My Fear of Marriage and Family

Every one of us will have crossroads in our journey of faith. God in His love knows when and how to challenge our hearts to change, always for our growth. One of my monumental crossroads came during a typical Sunday morning church service that began as ordinary as the ones before it, but that service had a drastic effect on my life.

That morning the pastor began to share a message called "Motherhood—It's a High Calling." When he read the Scripture, "*Has not the Lord made them one [speaking of a husband and wife]? In flesh and spirit, they are His. And why one? Because He was seeking a godly offspring [seed]. So guard yourself in your spirit and do not break faith with the wife of your youth*" (Mal. 2:15, bracketed copy mine), I began to weep immediately. I know that may sound odd, but it was as though something in the depths of my being began to shake and quiver on the inside. My heart began to pound, and I felt weak—too weak to fight it.

It would have been easy to believe that the pastor was directing his entire message to me as he spoke of motherhood and the calling to invest in children's lives. I was overwhelmed by how precious this calling is to God. How precious is the individual child! God knows every child and has a unique plan for his or her destiny. This may sound funny, but I began to realize that giving birth to and raising godly children was greater than protecting dolphins and endangered species—this was a high calling of God.

I felt as though I was the only one in the room, and my heart was being laid bare for everyone to see. Mothering children was an area of my life to which I had long since locked up and thrown away the key. After my parents had a short separation when I was around the age of ten, I had made an inner vow that I would never get married or have children. And that's what the female icons told me to do. Even my schoolteacher had given me a copy of the book *Girls Are Equal Too*, and I had tried to convince myself that marriage and kids would be a waste of my potential. I could do so much more in life without the burden. That was the lie I fed myself.

In reality, I was afraid of commitment—afraid of being hurt, rejected, and left alone. It was fear that held me to this vow, not self-ambition, and when my eyes were opened to this fact, I was overwhelmed. The hardened attitude that kids were brats and that abortion was a pest exterminator left me. I repented for them. I knew I was wrong to have ever believed the lies that had been fed to all of us young women. The truth was that we wanted to believe the lies in order to justify our "choices," our selfish motives. We had devoured the lies as though they were a seven-course meal, because we didn't believe a healthy marriage and family was possible.

> Stronger than all the evils in the soul is the Word, and the healing power that dwells in Him.
> ORIGEN

In that 40-minute sermon, my fear of marriage and children and the vulnerability of opening my heart dissipated. I wasn't sure where it went, but it left, and I was completely free. I accepted the truth that it was a high calling to have children. I knew that day I would get married and have children one day…and for the first time in my life, I actually invited the thought. *That was revolutionary!*

I didn't know what to call it that day, but I had received emotional healing from the fear of rejection. I was now free to explore options in my life that I had never allowed myself to think were possible. I found that so many of my other life decisions up until that point had also been based on fear. The longer I lived in the Kingdom of God, the more I was challenged with other areas in my life where I had allowed fear to dominate me. I discovered there were many fears that had held me as a hostage—the fear of failure, the fear of being rejected or the fear of man, the fear of death, the fear of being alone—and I wondered how many others were bound by similar fears.

The Fear of the Lord

I had to learn the difference between wisdom and fear. Wisdom is for my protection. To have a healthy "fear of the Lord" is a good thing according to the Word of God. *"Behold, the reverential and worshipful fear of the Lord—that is Wisdom; and to depart from evil is understanding"* (Job 28:28 AMP). What is this type of reverential fear? It is an understanding that God is the Supreme Authority over the entire universe, and there are choices I make that will have temporal as well as eternal consequences.

In my new freedom, I also discovered that God's rules for right and wrong, which I had set aside, were really God's ways of protecting me from the pain I had experienced and the fears I had lived under. Now I found that my heart wanted to learn His ways that bring and keep me under His protection with the promises of peace, joy, prosperity, and long life.

King Solomon said, *"Do not be wise in your own eyes; fear the Lord and shun evil. This will bring health to your body and nourishment to your bones"* (Prov. 3:7–8). There is a connection between our attitudes and actions and the outcomes in our lives, including our health. *"A man reaps what he sows"* is a principle at work in every area of our lives (see Gal. 6:7). The fear of the Lord means we build our lives upon and around the Word of God (the Scriptures), because we respect that God's ways are the right ways and result in health to our lives. If we sow to the Spirit, we reap abundant life. If we sow to the flesh (or earth-cursed system), we reap corruption.

God's Kingdom is set up in such a way to train, teach, and mentor us into making choices that are the most beneficial for others and for us. It is based in love. All of the Ten Commandments are about "protecting love," not hurting others for our own gain. Jesus said He came to fulfill the commandments because He is love. He is not trying to hurt us or rule us with an iron fist. Remember, He is the Designer, and He knows how the design works—what will make you and me flourish according to how we were created. He even knows every detail about the pain and the deficits in our lives from being born into and raised in the earth-cursed system, and He knows how to free us from their grip.

To fear putting our hand on a hot stove is to respect the stove. It is wise to choose to not do certain things. God's Word and His Spirit who lives within us give us the wisdom to know what choices to make. "*Do your best to present yourself to God as one approved, a workman who does not need to be ashamed and who correctly handles the word of truth*" (2 Tim. 2:15). The more we know about His Kingdom, the freer we become! "*You will know the truth, and the truth will set you free*" (John 8:32).

With freedom, there is responsibility. This is simple truth, but you would be surprised how many people I encounter, particularly women, who know truth but make decisions based on their emotions rather than the Kingdom of God. They want to live in the promises of the King without following His principles or decrees. If we don't know the truth, we're ignorant; but if we know the truth and disregard it, we are disobedient. Disobedience will not bring forth the fruit or outcomes of God's Kingdom in our lives.

Wisdom is readily available to us through the Word of God, the counsel of experienced leaders whom God has placed in the Kingdom, and by prayer in the Holy Spirit. At least two and hopefully all three will have the same report of agreement. Human leadership is fallible, but the Word of God and the Holy Spirit are not. Jesus said, *"Each tree is recognized by its own fruit"* (Luke 6:44), and you can recognize godly leadership by the model, teachings, and outcomes in their own lives.

> Without good direction, people lose their way; the more wise counsel you follow, the better your chances
> (PROVERBS 11:14 MSG).

If a spiritual leader warns or corrects you, then do not proceed ahead. Step back, pray, and seek God until it is clear that the direction is absolutely confirmed as God's direction. Ask yourself, does it line up with the Scriptures? Who will it affect? Is it honest? Does it match the pattern of love?

I have seen believers take many false steps because they think they can follow God without any counsel and disregard any type of leadership in their lives. Remember, satan masquerades as an angel of light (see 2 Cor. 7:14), and he is seeking those whom he may devour (see 1 Pet. 5:8). Freedom doesn't mean that I don't submit myself or come under the loving protection of a spiritual leader. Yes, we can be led by the King and follow His decrees from His Word, but we tend to get caught up in the emotion of the moment, so it is wise to have spiritual mothers and fathers who have lived long enough to understand the tactics satan uses to ensnare believers to entice them out of the Kingdom or to make them ineffective in the Kingdom. *"Resist him, standing firm in the faith"* (1 Pet. 5:9).

One of my favorite Scriptures is *"Be steadfast, immovable, always abounding in the work of the Lord"* (1 Cor. 15:58 NKJV). For any major direction that I am going to take in life, I try to get good counsel (often from my husband or additional seasoned believers), and I base my decisions on the Word of God and leadership. *"By the mouth of two or three witnesses every word shall be established"* (Matt. 18:16 NKJV). If it is contrary to the teachings of the Bible, God's instruction book for life, then it is not God. He does not violate His Word or go back on it.

The fear of the Lord involves a healthy respect for the consequences of bad decisions and an expectancy of promises gained for right choices.

Dealing With Fear

With any other encountered fear, besides the fear of the Lord, I have learned to deal with it as destructive. *"For God has not given us a spirit of fear, but of power and of love and of a sound mind"* (2 Tim. 1:7). God is not the author of fear, and before Adam and Eve made the decision to disobey (before the earth curse), there was only one regulation, *"You must not eat from the tree of the knowledge of good and evil, for when you eat of it you will surely die"* (Gen. 2:17). What a simple life. No curses, no pain, no problems, no death, and a beautiful earth all around to enjoy.

Adam and Eve had it all, but they became convinced by the enemy that they were missing something, that God had withheld the best from them. It seems as though most of the wrong decisions I've made started with a curiosity, a longing for something I thought I was missing, even though God says, "*His divine power has given us everything we need for life and godliness through our knowledge of Him who called us by His own glory and goodness*" (2 Peter 1:3). In Adam and Eve's case…and in our cases, if we trust God's love for us, then we don't have to fear being left out or left behind or even death itself. "*There is no fear in love. But perfect love drives out fear, because fear has to do with punishment. The one who fears is not made perfect in love*" (1 John 4:18). As we grasp His love, fear departs, and peace reigns.

I have found the way to overcome lies and temptations is through knowing and recognizing the truth of God's Word. If I can replace every lie with truth, I will not be led away into temptation and the bondages that come into my life when I make wrong choices. If I am complete in God's love, I don't fear being rejected. I must counter the earth-curse fears and lies with the new truth from the Kingdom. In all kinds of situations throughout the years, I have asked myself, "What does God have to say about this?" The Holy Spirit will actually lead us to the answer right in the Word of God, and He always makes a way to escape the corruption of the world's system (see 1 Cor. 10:13). I must heed it, but the answer is there.

Some of the fears we experience are so deep rooted from trauma and lies we have believed for so long that they have become strongholds in our lives. God did not bring evil to us to teach us. He cannot, for there is no evil in His character. He does not tempt us with evil, but rather the Bible says we are tempted by our own inner desires and lusts (see James 1:14). What we hide, God cannot heal. Again, the Word of God is our key to tearing down strongholds.

Once we have established our stand of freedom, we are instructed to give no place to the enemy in our lives—to not reopen any door to him. Our disobedience invites demonic activity to move into situations in our lives. Once you are free, slam the door on the past—the sin, the disobedience, and fear—and keep it shut.

The ultimate test of every spiritual battle is: If it brings real life, then we can credit it to God. If it has any element of theft, death, or destruction, then we know the earth curse and satan are at work, and we can also resist it because we know it is not an act of God, but rather the enemy. Jesus said, "*The thief does not come except to steal, and to kill, and to destroy. I have come that they may have life, and that they may have it more abundantly*" (John 10:10 NKJV). Jesus

> Above all, if we would successfully resist Satan, we must look not merely to revealed wisdom but to Incarnate Wisdom. We must flee to Him "who has become for us wisdom from God—that is, our righteousness, holiness and redemption" (1 Corinthians 1:30). He must teach us, He must guide us, He must be All-in-all. The sheep are never so safe from the wolf as when they are near the Shepherd.
> CHARLES SPURGEON

has redeemed us from the curse of the law or the earth-cursed system, so we do not have to stay under the pressures of that system. And He has rendered the work of satan powerless against our lives, so we do not have to live under the enemy's oppression any longer. We just have to learn our rights as a citizen in God's Kingdom and enforce them for our complete freedom.

The woman who has "IT" realizes the choice comes down to her knowledge of the King, His Kingdom, and her obedience to live in freedom.

Truly Free

After the God-encounter I had about my womanhood and the

changed attitudes toward motherhood, I felt a desire to go on to college, but I chose a Christian college instead of my previous plans. My pastor and his wife encouraged me to go and helped me figure out how to afford it. It was there I met Gary, a shy, tenderhearted, set-in-his-ways bachelor who was 26 years old. We also worked part time together at a window treatment store, where I sold the window coverings and he installed them. (We joke today that I am still selling vision that he has to install!)

Although I went to college to get away from relationships and to focus on developing my relationship with God, when I met Gary the first time, I had a sense of something special. He had a Tootsie Roll Pop in his mouth, a head full of bushy curly hair, and wore a plaid flannel shirt and a pair of corduroys. He smiled awkwardly and didn't say anything but "Hey." When he spoke, the thought came to me from seemingly nowhere, *Is he the one?* I chided myself and even resisted the thought, saying to myself, "You've only just met him! You don't even know him," but time proved to me that this thought had been a probing of the Holy Spirit, later confirmed by my pastor and family. My mother said the first time she met Gary she knew he was my husband.

I grew to respect Gary's devotion to God and his easygoing personality. He was the opposite end of the spectrum from the driven lifestyle I had operated under, and I found him comforting. He would see me at work and say, "You're a real sweetheart," and then he would smile sheepishly and look away. We had not dated, but we went to a small country church a few times together, and one of those times he brought a friend along. (I found out later he did it so I wouldn't figure out that he liked me, but I already knew that.) Because he was shy, and I wasn't, he wasn't sure how to navigate this relationship. One day, God spoke to him that I was to be his wife, and he later proposed to me on a sunny Tulsa spring afternoon.

I felt certain of my answer to this tender man I had grown to respect, so I said, "Yes, but you must first meet Pastor Vic for his approval." Because insecurity had caused me to be fickle on so many occasions, I did not completely trust myself, and I didn't want to marry the wrong person. I felt Gary was to be my husband, but I wanted him to meet my pastor back home for his confirmation and approval. I had promised God, more for my own reassurance, I would do this, so I would know once and forever that he was the one.

Pastor Vic immediately liked Gary. He was uncomplicated, humble, tender, and read the Bible more than anyone I knew. And he loved me.

Pastor Vic asked me, "Drenda, why do you feel Gary is your husband?"

I said, "He is the first man I have ever *wanted* to submit to."

Pastor Vic laughed and said, "I believe he is your husband." Those were the words I had told God I needed to hear to be sure. I have never doubted those words, even though we have had some hurdles to climb in our marriage.

Of all the adventures I have experienced, the love of my husband and the joy of motherhood to five children are the richest I could ever imagine.

get Marriage:
EXPERIENCE LASTING LOVE

What Is Your "Reflection"?

The Right Foundation for Marriage

Replacement Thinking

Respect

Living by the One Team Concept

Talk His Language

4 get Marriage:

EXPERIENCE
LASTING LOVE

In marriage, being the right person is
as important as finding the right person.
Wilbert Donald Gough

In the beginning of our marriage, even though God had done a real work in my heart, I was still very insecure and had many moments of doubt. As we drove home to Tulsa from our East Coast mountain-to-beach honeymoon, my younger brother passed away after a battle with cancer, which created new hurts and feelings of separation for me that neither Gary nor I understood. Even though I knew cancer, not God, had taken my brother away, I felt angry, and the disappointment caused fresh doubts to surface.

Occasionally, the fears would come back, and I would give in to their attacks. Just a few months into our marriage, overcome by these feelings, I got in our car and drove to an empty parking lot at our alma mater. With my head on the steering wheel, through sobs I cried, "God, I can do anything, but marriage." It was an entirely new challenge, and I just couldn't seem to handle it. Everything I had done in school prepared me for a career, but very little had prepared me for marriage. Pastor Vic had given me a biblical basis and understanding of marriage, but I knew I had to choose to live it. I prayed, submitting my will, and drove home.

To add to the pressure, besides the intense financial strain of learning how to live on a commissioned income, I became pregnant with our first child just six months after we married. My past beliefs about marriage and children had changed, but I suddenly felt so vulnerable, and my trust in God and Gary was tested. We were thrilled when I originally found I was pregnant, but four months into the pregnancy I felt insecure about the changes in my body and my ability to make it *alone*—if Gary were to up and leave me.

"Why would I even think such a thing?" I asked myself. But then voices from my past kicked back in. "How can you be sure he's not like so many other men?"

I started meditating on these fears, then dropped hints in conversations with Gary that I needed reassurance, but he didn't read between the lines. Irrationally, I convinced myself he must not love me. Alone in our apartment one spring evening, I grabbed a couple of suitcases and met him at our second-story apartment door when he arrived home from work. He said, "What are you doing?" I hurled the first accusation that came to my mind, "You don't love me, and I'm going back home to my parents." (It seemed to work in the movies, so why not on my husband?)

Gary seemed unsure as to how to respond, but finally he managed, "What will you do for money? Don't you need a credit card or something?"

This was not exactly the reassurance I was looking for! I was angry now. Unable to hide my hurt, I teared up. Then he softened and with tears of his own, he said, "Can we talk about this tonight and see if you still feel the same way tomorrow?" He didn't know that my bags were actually empty. I was just searching to

locate his heart. His tender words and thoughtfulness that evening melted me. He gave me all the reassurance that his love for
me was only stronger as we took on the new
venture of parenting together.

> I suspect that in every
> good marriage there
> are times when love
> seems to be over.
> MADELEINE L'ENGLE

I have tested Gary's love for me over and
over again, but he has always managed to
work through my fears. We have learned
through the years to be there for each other. There have been
other times when he needed my comfort and encouragement,
too. We have both gone through tough times and managed to
keep our love growing—not perfectly, but learning together.

What Is Your "Reflection"?

There are many reasons people are not enjoying the love God
intended them to experience in this life. Besides the importance
of an introduction to the One who created love as the first and
foremost basis for love, we need to understand how we were
created as women and men as well as the negative effects of the
earth-cursed system on our relationships and how to overcome
them.

As women, we were made "to reflect" something. Whether we
accept it or not, our created purpose as documented in the Book
of Genesis was to be "a helper" for man, to come alongside him
and be a companion and support (see Gen. 2:18). In that we
were created with this purpose in mind, to rebel against it is a
road to self-denial and pain. The earth curse brought a new twist
on this created purpose, and our reflection became muddled.

Many single women I speak with who are very successful in their
careers express their desires for a "man to love" and a family.

I meet women who are happily and unhappily married, and women who wish they were married but haven't found "love." Some of them are infatuated with their bosses, co-workers, married men, and even pastors. I have to help them keep the perspective that it is possible to be married and unhappy as well as to be single and happy. Our station in life, whatever it is, is not where we derive our worth or identity or happiness.

The question is, where are we getting our "reflection"? We can get our reflection from our husbands, our children, our careers, our volunteer work, or any number of other achievements, pursuits, and people in our lives. But these are all temporal. As sad as it is, husbands can walk away from marriages or tragically pass away. Children grow up and leave our nest to pursue their own lives, as they should. Careers can come and go, especially in today's economy. Friends may lose interest or move away. And while achievements are wonderful, if our reflection is completely based on them, we must always be achieving more or we sink into a deep feeling of low self-worth.

A woman who has "IT" realizes that relationships and things, in and of themselves, can't make her happy, but she has the power to bring happiness to her relationships if she chooses—and that includes her marriage.

The Right Foundation for Marriage

To have a truly successful marriage, we have to start on the right foundation for marriage. Is our understanding of marriage from God's Word or from the world? In the Book of Genesis, woman was created as a reflection of man. She was made to reflect his glory. She was taken from him and given back to him to be a source of companionship, great comfort, and delight (see Gen. 2:20–24). She was also created equally with man in the likeness and image of God (see Gen. 1:27).

If a woman's identity is totally lost in her relationship with her husband, she will always try to pull something from him that he is unable to provide. She is a reflection of her "man," not the man himself. When women try to find their entire worth from the opinion or love of a man, they are both going to be miserable. A man can never give her enough reassurance of her worth and identity. Researchers say that a woman may need as many as 22 affirmations of love a day! She can reflect her husband's care for her, but even that is a tall order for any man.

First Corinthians 11:3–15 states that Jesus Christ is a reflection of the Father, man is a reflection of Christ, and the woman is the reflection of the man. For our purposes, I am quoting only verses 3, 7–9, and 11–12.

> *Now I want you to realize that the head of every man is Christ, and the head of the woman is man, and the head of Christ is God. A man ought not to cover his head, since he is the image and glory of God; but the woman is the glory of man. For man did not come from woman, but woman from man; neither was man created for woman, but woman for man. In the Lord, however, woman is not independent of man, nor is man independent of woman. For as woman came from man, so also man is born of woman. But everything comes from God.*

We hear people say "I don't need a man" or "I don't need women." But we can't be totally independent of each other! No doubt, there has been a lot of misunderstanding between men and women concerning their need for each other and how to get along together. Try as we may to denounce our mutual needs, it's not possible.

But is it really possible for a man and a woman to have a fulfilling relationship with each other? I believe the answer is a resounding "Yes!" God's ultimate plan was that this completeness with each other would be found in Him and expressed in the marriage covenant.

> Chains do not hold a marriage together. It is threads, hundreds of tiny threads which sew people together through the years.
>
> SIMONE SIGNORET

We need to understand the nature of the relational problem. First, we know that our negative reflection of ourselves originated from The Fall. Second, we know that the earth curse put us under subjection to a fruitless cycle of insanity, where a woman is always trying to get her identity from a man who at the same time is trying to get his identity from his work and tends to rule over her in the process. In this system, he isn't helped, because he "rules" over her instead of working along with her. He isn't aware of her needs, because his needs are different, and he is busy trying to make a living. She is not fulfilled, because she is pulling on him for something he is neither willing nor focused toward giving to her. Emulating his example, she pursues other interests, trying to fulfill her needs with children or a career or, sometimes, another lover.

What a vicious setup for failure in any relationship! The earth curse upon the woman says, "*Your desire will be for your husband, and he will rule over you*" (Gen. 3:16). To the man the curse included working in a system that would never produce enough for him to rest. He would labor until death and experience sorrow all his days, trying to provide from a system that was broken. Meanwhile, his wife would make him feel unappreciated in the process, and they would both become bitter and resentful.

To further complicate this picture, we women carry into marriage our past experiences of men whom we have tried to derive our identity from since early childhood. A father is a girl's first reflection of who she is and her worth. Little girls will do just about anything to get the love and attention of their daddies. Daddy has a very special place in a girl's heart. This obviously has a positive side to it, but the negative side is that if a young woman never experiences the love, protection, and affirmation of her father, she will carry that deficit outside of her home to another man's doorstep, which puts her in a very vulnerable position.

Men have learned from the earth-cursed system how to manipulate this for their own selfish gain. Thus, the mantra that we hear so often from women: "We have given ourselves to men, and they abused us—emotionally, sexually, and physically." If that begins in the home relationship with a girl's father, as has happened in so many women's lives, she will carry the baggage and perceptions forward from one man to another, and the pain will heighten with each breakup cycle and so will the insecurity.

Throughout history, women and children from all over the world have been the victims of abuse. One in four women in America will become a victim of domestic violence. Nearly 17,000 people, mainly women, are killed each year by an intimate partner, according to the National Coalition of Domestic Violence. Contrary to popular belief, wherever Christianity has dominated the "conscience" of a nation, women have been elevated to a higher place of respect and protection. Abuse of women or children is inconsistent with the teachings or example of Jesus or the Scriptures. "*There is neither...male nor female, for you are all one in Christ Jesus*" (Gal. 3:28). Both are co-heirs with Christ in this life and have equal standing in the eyes and heart of God (see Rom. 8:17); they only differ in design and function.

How are a man and woman co-heirs in marriage? He carries the ultimate responsibility and must love his wife "*as Christ loved the church and gave Himself up for her*" (Eph. 5:25). She is the one who "*must respect her husband*" and get behind his leadership (Eph. 5:33). Where he goes, so does she. And if they go without each other, they will grow apart and miss out on the reward of enjoying their dreams and successes as a team. Men are to lead, much like the CEO of the family, and women are to reap the benefits of the company as a co-laborer and valuable co-owner. It's like stock options; if we work together, we both get paid the same on our stock, even though he's the CEO or head.

> The best marriages, like the best lives, were both happy and unhappy. There was even a kind of necessary tension, a certain tautness between the partners that gave the marriage strength, like the tautness of a full sail. You went forward on it.
>
> ANNE MORROW LINDBERGH

A wife shouldn't have to bear the weighty responsibility of the lead role, and the husband shouldn't have to fight to get her on-board. If some people behaved at work in the same manner they treat their spouse, they would be fired on the spot. Why can we give the proper respect in the workplace but fail to do so in the home?

Both men and women have a tendency to revert back to the earth curse. When men and women use each other, they both lose. Women use the need men have for respect and a physical release through the act of sex to get what they want from men. For her, the payoff is oftentimes either in the form of meeting emotional needs or financial needs. But she doesn't get what she truly needs if she manipulated the man to get it.

Men and women have been playing these games since the beginning of time, blaming each other for the problems and breakdowns in their relationships. What they're doing is misusing each other to try to fix the earth curse in themselves. He's thinking sex and work, and she's thinking desire for his time and attention, which she believes means love. It's time to stop blaming each other and start understanding each other and ourselves.

Replacement Thinking

When we understand the needs of our marriage partner and sincerely desire to meet those needs by God's grace and help, then a real joy in the relationship can result. But men or women cannot completely meet each other's needs. Our identity first has to come with identifying with the work of Jesus Christ on the cross, restoring us to a place where we are daughters and sons of God. We must derive our reflection from God. When we know His love, forgiveness, and acceptance as His children, we then have something to offer to someone else. "*Freely you have received, freely give*" (Matt. 10:8). As God's children, we can give love because we have received love.

The woman who has "IT" recognizes "who" she is in Christ apart from any other relationship.

With that as my basis, any time in a relationship when I feel let down or start to struggle with feelings of unworthiness, I trace it back to the origin. *When did I start to feel this way? What happened?*

What was said or done that brought me to this wrong conclusion? I can almost always find an event or situation where I was looking to get my security from something that is temporary, and it didn't go the way I wanted it to go, so I felt a sense of rejection or a lack of "positive reflection." I am not reflecting anything positive, because my thoughts are negative. Instead, I reflect the thought I have allowed to permeate my thinking: *I'm not loved. Everyone's too busy for me. I'm getting older, and there's no value in my life.* All lies (except we are getting older), but if you or I allow ourselves to continue to think negative thoughts such as these, they become messages we believe, because we drew conclusions from temporary events!

Oftentimes, though, we are building a case against ourselves that we have already decided is true. If we hold deep-seated beliefs that we "are" rejected, unloved, or unworthy, we will filter all of our experiences with people and situations through these negative beliefs. The more we build negative evidence, the more we become convinced it must be true. If we are to ever have a lasting, meaningful relationship with ourselves or anyone else, we have to stop these destructive thought patterns. If we maintain unhealthy views of who we are, we are more than likely going to open ourselves up to unhealthy relationships with destructive patterns.

The way I deal with myself in these situations is to first isolate the situation and the negative thought that came with it, much as a doctor diagnoses a problem. Cause and effect in mind, I replace the negative thought or conclusion with a promise from my Father—a promise from His Word that I know I can trust because He never lets me down. Whether people come through for me or not, He always does! Whether someone likes me, loves me, or hates me, He loves me. So I must be lovable! If His love is there for me, I am worthy of love. Case closed.

Sometimes it helps to memorize or write out several Scriptures that reaffirm His love, healing, or provision for us. Whatever the situation, there is a promise in the form of a Scripture we can replace our negative thought with and move forward with a renewed sense of well-being. I have reinvented my life with this type of replacement thinking. A friend of mine says, "Jesus got an A on His report card, and we got an F, but since He took my F to the cross, I get His A." Even if I did really blow it in a situation, and I deserve punishment, I can renew my heart with the knowledge that I am loved, because He first loved me, when I didn't deserve it and couldn't earn it.

Then I am free to say, "I'm sorry. I was wrong," and even make restitution to someone else, without feeling like a loser who has to do penance before I can accept I am lovable again. I can forgive myself immediately, and I am free to love those around me. *I don't use my vacuum of neediness to suck the life out of people.* Instead, I become a water hose, showering others with love. I can love others, even troublesome people, because I am truly confident, happy, and less self-focused. I can look at people with eyes of love and overlook their faults and not be concerned about whether they treat me well or not. I'm at peace, and I'm not easily shaken by the darts of hurting people. Hurting people really do hurt people, but only if we allow it. This isn't an arrogant attitude; it is merely recognizing the value and priority God places on each of us as worthy enough for Christ to die for us.

> A happy marriage is the union of two good forgivers.
> RUTH BELL GRAHAM

When someone does wrong to us, we can truly forgive him or her, because we have received forgiveness. By making allowance for imperfections, we can give them the mercy and consideration we have received and release us both from judgmental attitudes. If we look for them to make us happy, we are both going to be miserable. If we can be content with "who" we are and that we are growing in God's grace, then we can extend the same consideration to others.

Respect

You may ask, "What does respect have to do with relationships and marriage?" *Everything!* I make myself "ready" for a relationship when I no longer seek it just to satisfy myself, but rather I am so full of the love I have received from God that now I want to give it away. This is true of friendships and romantic relationships. I can forgive, accept our differences, and not place unrealistic expectations on the relationship. The woman with "IT" knows she cannot get happiness from another person, but can only give "IT" when she has "IT."

Keep in mind that the best marriages are built upon friendship. Above everything else in our marriage, Gary and I are friends. We have learned how to love each other, to meet each other's needs, but we are friends first. It started that way and keeps growing deeper as we walk through new seasons of life together, hand in hand and heart to heart. We don't always agree on everything, we don't always do what we should, but we each know that we are committed to always being there for each other.

Respect is a large part of our love. I respect the pressures upon him to provide, protect, lead, and love our family and me. He understands that I need reassurance of his love through verbal communication and time when he is focused on me and the family. I want the security of his love for life, and he needs to know that I am always there for him and I respect him. It is very comforting and reassuring to us both as we face outside pressures and dream about and create the future together.

No ambition or desire takes the place of our first commitment to love each other. Gary and I are committed to growing old together. The day before our wedding, a note attached to yellow roses from Gary read, "Looking forward to spending the rest of my life with you." We have shared this phrase back and forth since then. He has honored his commitment through all the ups and downs, and I respect him for it.

More than anything, husbands need respect from their wives. Typically in relationships, we meet someone we respect and think we would like to have their love and commitment, but once we have it, we tend to disrespect them later if we don't get what we want. When that happens with our husbands, too often we punish them with our words and by withholding sex to show them how unhappy we are. This is very dangerous and the first step to destroying the marriage. "*The wise woman builds her house, but with her own hands the foolish one tears hers down*" (Prov. 14:1). Women who have "IT" understand that men need to have a supportive friend in a wife who builds him up, believes in him, and, foremost, respects him.

It is an interesting analogy that a husband is to love his wife as Christ loves the church and gave Himself up for her to present her as a glorious bride; and a wife is to reverence and respect her husband, submitting to (meaning to "come under the protection") of his love (see Eph. 5:22–33). Jesus wants His followers to believe in Him; a husband wants his wife to believe in him!

First Peter 3:1–7 instructs:

> *Wives, in the same way be submissive to your husbands so that, if any of them do not believe the word, they may be won over without words by the behavior of their wives, when they see the purity and reverence of your lives. Your beauty should not come from outward adornment, such as braided hair and the wearing of gold jewelry and fine clothes. Instead, it should be that of your inner self, the unfading beauty of a gentle and quiet spirit, which is of great worth in God's sight. For this is the way the holy women of the past who put their hope in God used to make themselves beautiful. They were submissive to their own husbands, like Sarah, who obeyed Abraham and called him her master. You are her daughters if you do what is right and do not give way to fear. Husbands, in the same way be considerate as you live with your wives, and treat them with respect as the weaker partner and as heirs with you of the gracious gift of life, so that nothing will hinder your prayers.*

This marriage process takes faith, and we only stick with it when we do not give way to fear. The rewards of the Lord are about staying in the process! It's not always easy to live, but we are placing our trust not just in our mate, but also in God Himself. I have seen many relationships healed and restored because one or both spouses got a right picture of the design for marriage from God's Word and began to live it in love before the other spouse. This is not as a means to manipulate, but rather as a way to win their heart. We must replace our fear of commitment with faith and keep the picture of God's Word in front of us by faith instead of our feelings. Feelings can be very fickle and deceptive, but not if we anchor them to God's Word and the picture or outcome His Word paints for us as we follow Him. We cannot let feelings dictate our decisions. We must "decide" based on God's design for life, and then we can enjoy the positive feelings that come from the rewards of following His ways.

Gary and I have been self-employed our entire married life, so at times we have had feasting and famine. When we first started a business, after expenses, we did not have a profit margin for several years. Our overhead was low, and we were advanced commissions on sales, so we had enough to live on, but no profits. Even so, I was certain we needed to pay taxes, but Gary thought that if we didn't have profits, we had no tax liability. Three years into our business, he discovered that we did indeed owe self-employment taxes. When he called me with the bad news of not only the back taxes but also the penalties we owed because of his mistake, I could hear fear and disappointment in his voice.

> There is nothing more lovely in life than the union of two people whose love for each other has grown through the years from the small acorn of passion to a great rooted tree. Surviving all vicissitudes, and rich with its manifold branches, every leaf holding its own significance.
>
> VITA SACKVILLE-WEST

I was about to remind him how I had told him so, but before I could get the words out, the Holy Spirit checked me in my spirit. I swallowed hard and changed my thoughts to Gary's needs instead of mine. I wanted to vindicate myself and reiterate my past warnings, proving I was right, but Gary needed me. So I humbled myself, took a deep breath, and said, "Honey, it is going to be all right. It's just a mistake, and we can overcome it. I believe in you, and things are going to get better." And they did.

Years later, we are enjoying the fruit of working as a team. We have raised five children who love God and us, have built three companies, have paid for our home, and have no debt. Our hearts have the same mission to help others as we minister in our church, on television, and in materials. I love my life, but we have the outcome of God's design by following His ways instead of our own path of selfishness.

Living by the One Team Concept

A great anointing of God's Spirit or presence is released when a wife has faith in God and faith in her husband. There are many times we can take each other "to the cleaners" within a marriage, but when we realize what is at stake, we don't do it. What do we gain? No one wins when we fight for our own rights and try to prove we know more.

I call this "competing" with our husbands. We were designed to complete them and work with them, not to be a competitor. It took Gary and me many years to realize we were not competing against each other, because we were both afraid to trust. When we came to understand the "one team concept" (which we did by humbling ourselves in love), we began to draw on each other's strengths rather than waste time arguing. Gary learned that he could ask me my opinions without feeling threatened, and I learned to communicate them to him without making him feel disrespected. We honored the differences and the viewpoint each of us brought to the "table."

I compare our relationship to epoxy glue. The two elements that make up epoxy lack strength alone. But when you combine the two, a unique chemistry takes place and the compounds, although different, take on a strength that is almost unbreakable. "*Two are better than one, because. . .if one falls down, his friend can help him up*" (Eccles. 4:9–10). We try to lift each other up and genuinely care how the other person feels, and we desire to succeed together as a team. I know Gary is seeking my best interests, and he knows that I am guarding our love and relationship.

If wives act virtuously in marriage, the Bible says our husbands will praise us in the city gates (see Prov. 31:31)! Gary thanks me often for helping to make him successful. I laugh because I appreciate his willingness to credit me, even though I spent the first part of our marriage trying to "put him in his place," and he reciprocated by indifference. Now we are trying to see the contribution each has made to our life together, preferring each other in love. Only God's love in a marriage can bring a couple to a place of understanding that "oneness" can be achieved. "*And the two will become one flesh*" (Mark 10:8). The act of sexual intimacy may bring a couple into physical oneness, but only the act of laying down our lives for each other can bring a couple to a place of spiritual unity, *true oneness.*

Gary says he has learned that if I start to get negative or critical, he needs to invest some time and love into me. He says that it is up to him to make me a radiant bride, so that I reflect his love. If the reflection isn't right, he takes the responsibility to invest and find out why. If your husband isn't at that place, remember that a great marriage is built over time, not delivered on the first day or even in the first ten years. Our relationship was not always there either. Don't give up! Every disagreement and misunderstanding we have endured was worth it to enjoy the fruit of life together we are now experiencing.

I have learned that my husband can't assume responsibility for my complete happiness. When he takes the first step to love me, it causes me to analyze if it is our relationship or my relationship with

God that has a deficit. My struggle is often a spiritual need that I am trying to get met in our relationship or in some way other than God. This drives me back to my priorities and keeps me honest with myself. I must keep returning to God and His love to be able to be content. If Eve was not content in a perfect world, we can make trouble in the best of situations with the kindest husband if we fail to place our expectations and identity in the Lord.

I remind myself often *"A gracious woman retains honor"* (Prov. 11:16 NKJV). Men have a code of honor that dictates they would die for their family. If he is willing to physically die for honor, then surely I can give up some of my attitudes and pride and die to my demands to have my way. I want to be gracious, slow to anger, and kind in my words and deeds to my family, and especially to my husband. Besides that, our children are learning life from us.

When we give honor to our husbands, even when it sometimes doesn't look as though they deserve it, we honor Christ and God's plan, so even the harsh or negative husband can be won without words by our godly actions. If we invest or give honor, we receive it. God will see to it in the long term. Ultimately, as we honor God's ways, He is able to move in the relationship. The most hard-hearted men have been won over, and for those who retain evil, God has dealt with them as well, as seen in the story of Abigail and King David (see 1 Sam. 25). I have seen this play out in the lives of faithful women. God is our ultimate source and protection.

Of course, neither you nor your children should ever be physically abused! Separate and get help emotionally and, when necessary, legally. But even abuse has taken on a new twist or definition. I have met women and men who tell me they are getting a divorce because of "incompatability" or that their mate is "abusive." When I ask about the abuse, it is often nothing more than a disagreement or a clash of wills. Just because two people disagree or have an argument does not mean "abuse" was involved. Instead of getting counsel and learning proper ways to communicate, they just want out of the marriage. Often they have already eyed another person they are interested in or think the grass will be greener with someone else. Every relationship has challenges, and every person has strengths and weaknesses, as evidenced in the failure rate of second and third marriages. We just exchange one set of problems for another instead of dealing with the real issues in our lives.

God hates divorce (see Mal. 2:16), and there is no wonder why. I have counseled with many couples and families. I have heard the tales of adultery from hurt women and men. I have held children and teens in my arms as they sobbed uncontrollably because their parents called it quits. I have seen the hatred in a young man's face whose father walked out on the family. I know the fears, the brokenness that children feel when their homes are torn apart and the security of home and love is divided. I hear adults talk of their "new relationships" and "new families," as if families were toys to be disposed of and new ones purchased. I've heard the heartbreak from children who have to see their "new" stepsiblings at school, knowing that their dad is now living with them instead. Men and women may find "new loves," but I have yet to see any of their children not have a living scar, a deep wound for life. I believe we will give the greatest account to God for how we handled the first priority of our marriage and families.

I remember as a young child that the prevailing attitude of most couples was to fight to stay together instead of look for a reason to part. Marriage was still viewed as worthwhile, and the respect it was given as an institution meant it was valuable and worth the effort. Then drastic changes began to happen, and as the fight for women's equality in every arena of life became almost a rebellion, marriages started failing by the thousands. No longer did either party stick it out, but both bailed out. This attitude has all but overtaken marriage, until we see a more than half failure rate today. Not to mention, a large percentage of couples are cohabiting and refusing to enter a marriage covenant.

> The heart of marriage is its communication system. It can be said that the success and happiness of any married pair is measurable in terms of the deepening dialogue which characterizes their union.
>
> DWIGHT SMALL

The woman who has "IT" will do whatever is within her power to respect the marriage covenant as holy and non-disposable. She cannot control the decisions of others, but she can control hers. It all comes back to mutual respect and respect for God's design and function for men and women. First, we respect God and His plan, and then it's easier to learn to respect each other.

Talk His Language

How does a woman respect her husband in an age where we have been taught to disrespect men in general? For me, it always starts with attitude and value. When we value something, we invest into it, and we don't mind making allowances and concessions to have mutual admiration and respect for its worth. When speaking to my husband, every time I think "love," I consider "honor" or "respect" instead. I have learned to tell my husband all the ways in which I respect him, and when I do this, I am talking his language. To a man, that's how we say "I love you." They see love as an "action," and we see it as a "feeling." A man shows his love by working and providing, by "doing something." They "respect" actions and want to be respected for their work ethic, courage, or good humor. A woman "feels" love and says it, usually in ways that females relate to more than men. Just as many men have great commitment to their love for their wives but struggle to say "I love you," women struggle to communicate their respect.

My husband says that it sends a man's brain into tilt when his wife wants him to *prove* he loves her. He equates his love for her to his work ethic and that he provides for her and returns to her again and again for sexual intimacy. In a more chivalrous time, it would be the same comparison as if he had just slain an enemy knight who was threatening his wife's life, and she turned to him and asked, "Do you love me?" *Tilt!*

Flowers and candy, romance and charming words are tougher for him to understand, but he can learn how to share his love for you in a language you understand, just as you can learn his vocabulary. The best way for him to learn is for you to be straightforward in your requests, without hints and hidden meanings. Just say what you want or need, with respect. Men do not read between the lines or jump to conclusions as women do. We hint, and they miss it, then we conclude they don't love us. Not fair, since we are speaking a language they don't get. This sends a man over the edge. I have learned to be straightforward when I communicate with Gary. I try not to hint and expect him to read between the lines as my female friends do. Instead, I tell him what I need or expect. He is usually more than happy to help.

All marriages have certain ways in which the couple learns to work and manage life together. There are no hard and fast rules except that they work together with a common goal to have a wonderful marriage, a healthy family, and fulfill their destiny as a family, providing training and security for the next generation.

In our home, Gary loves to fix breakfast and makes waffles for the kids and me almost every morning. In turn, I help him with business ideas and tackle travel plans for the family. Generally, women set the mood for the home and make it warm, attractive, and a pleasant place to come back to, and men provide for and protect the family. But this can take many forms as couples decide how they want to manage life and what they are each best gifted to help perform. It is all about honor and respect for what is important, not always getting our own way or "feeling" happy every day. Some days are tough. Marriage isn't always romantic, but through the thick and thin, the rewards are so worth it! Don't take your marriage or spouse for granted, for there are many who would gladly trade places with you. I have met them, and they almost always live with serious regrets.

I have learned it comes back to giving to our spouse "by faith." We cannot be complete unless we can receive and give love. If there is not an unconditional lifetime commitment to our marriage vow and partner, we will never feel the complete freedom to be ourselves in a relationship. Just as we receive God's gift of unconditional love to us, and it brings healing to our lives, a man and woman can bring healing to each other as they learn to love within God's plan and design for marriage.

One of the saddest scenes I have witnessed is a funeral at which the widow was crying with regret because she knew she had not expressed the respect she had for her husband, and it is too late. They wasted so many years arguing, trying to prove themselves right; in the end, no one wins. In some things we do not get a second chance. This is one of them.

get Intimacy
...get Sex:
NOT FOR SINGLES

Be Welded Together

Maintaining
the Passion

Within Marriage,
Sex Is Holy

Igniting Passion

The Song of Solomon

5
get Intimacy
...get Sex:
NOT FOR SINGLES

There is a tendency to think of sex as
something degrading; it is not, it is magnificent,
an enormous privilege, but because of that
the rules are tremendously strict.

Francis Devas

I caught you! Singles always turn to this chapter first! You may read it, but just don't put it into practice until you are in a marriage relationship.

Sex in the City is not as glamorous as many would have you to believe! In our nation alone the physical repercussions of a promiscuous lifestyle are taking a serious toll on men and women alike. There's been a great increase in sexually transmitted chlamydia infections—more than four times as many as 20 years ago—and still well over a million abortions a year in the United States. Not to mention the emotional pain of sharing such an intimate act with various partners.

One young woman told me she has had so many partners she has lost count. How sad. Since one-night stands have become a way of life for many singles, often the next step may be a "live-in" relationship that typically ends with a breakup and broken hearts. This supposed "love" can quickly turn into hurt and hate. If, and that's a big if, the relationship does result in marriage, it is most likely doomed, since it started on a wrong foundation, according to studies. Women are reportedly less happy with their lives in general and their love life than they were 10 and 20 years ago. One of the many attitudes that has changed is the attitude toward sex and commitment. The sexual revolution has resulted in the loss of a deeper understanding of true intimacy and oneness.

Every divorced woman whom I have talked with has told me that her marriage did not start on the right foundation. She compromised her spiritual standards and in many cases got involved sexually prior to the marriage union. This should be a warning to "*not be unequally yoked together with unbelievers*" (2 Cor. 6:14 NKJV) or someone who does not share our beliefs and values. If we want to have the blessing of the Lord, we need to keep our relationship right before Him. God's forgiveness and grace are greater than our mistakes, but why not do it right by His grace than have to deal with the problems that result from disobedience and loss of respect for each other. If he doesn't respect you enough to protect your purity prior to marriage, what makes you think he will respect you after marriage? It will take the same discipline and spiritual maturity to stay true to you as it took to stay true to God's ways prior to marriage.

Be a woman worthy of respect, and he will always hold you in higher esteem for your standard. What you compromise to gain, you ultimately lose. The best option is to avoid any opportunity to be in a situation where you may stumble. We have worked

with couples who have successfully remained pure by not being alone prior to marriage. They are together in their parents'
homes and in public gatherings, and they have siblings or friends
ride with them or go together with other couples. You can still
have intimate discussions and closeness in a park setting or restaurant. Accountability is the best way to keep passion in check
and not open any door to the adversary through wrongdoing.

Be Welded Together

I have come to understand that the marriage bed is the only
place where sexual intercourse is right, and anything else will
leave us feeling damaged and make it difficult to experience the
sexual intimacy with the partner God has for us. Every time we
give of ourselves to another person sexually, a piece of our heart
and very life goes from us. Repeated sexual encounters with
various partners compromise our heart and wholeness. "*Flee
[run] from sexual immorality. All other sins a man [or woman]
commits are outside his [or her] body, but he [or she] who sins sexually sins against his [or her] own body*" (1 Cor. 6:18, bracketed
copy mine). During sex, we exchange more than just a physical
experience; we become one with the person at the core of our
being spiritually.

The apostle Paul adds, "*Do you not know that your bodies
are members of Christ himself? Shall I then take the members
of Christ and unite them with a prostitute? Never! Do you not
know that he who unites himself with a prostitute is one with
her in body? For it is said, 'The two will become one flesh'*"
(1 Cor. 6:15–16). Those are some powerful words to consider.
There is a whole lot more shared in a sexual encounter than just
a casual night of fun. If you are having sex outside of marriage,
stop, repent, and renew your commitment to God's plan. It is

very possible to remain a virgin until your wedding night. If you are engaged or in a relationship you feel is leading into marriage, do not let your guard down until you say "I do." Many couples have rationalized that since they "know" marriage is forthcoming, it's OK to begin experimenting with sexual touches and even intercourse, but this will damage and could destroy the relationship before it ever begins. A large portion of the marriage problems I have counseled couples over could be traced back to the sexual activity they experienced prior to marriage. Stay pure and be a woman worthy of commitment and respect. Manipulating a man by using sex will always backfire, and you will ultimately regret it! Many are returning to this sacred view of sex. Read on, and you'll see why it's worth the wait.

Interestingly, God's second instruction to man and woman in the beginning of creation was how to relate in marriage. "*For this reason a man will leave his father and mother and be united to his wife, and they will become one flesh*" (Gen. 2:24). To *be united* means to "cleave" or "be welded" together. We are designed to be completely dependent on our spouse sexually. The man leaves his mother and father. They are no longer his primary focus, and he joins himself with his wife, becoming one flesh in a sexual union. The sexual exchange between a husband and wife is like oil that keeps their love fresh and tender and makes everything else in the marriage whole.

Maintaining the Passion

In the early years of our marriage, my desire was to please my husband in every way, including sexually, but as the children came and the busyness over the affairs of life began to consume our time, my desire for passion was often diminished. It is so easy to let our children and a busy schedule take away from the priority of our relationship with our spouse. Besides, I didn't feel as sexy with a "mommy body." We went to bed night after night, tired. We still had sex, but not as frequently, and my enthusiasm was not what it had been.

One night my husband confided in me that since we didn't make love as often as we once did, it had become a source of great temptation to him. His heart wanted to be true to me, but his need for sex caused him to feel drawn away. Initially, I was frustrated that he could even think about meeting his need any other way, but God began to deal with my heart on it. I could see that the frustration I was creating for my husband was much greater. Even though it was very difficult for him to bring it up, I was thankful he had come to me before anything serious had happened.

I realized that the sexual pressure he felt was a physical release that he needed, and I had failed to meet it. I told Gary how very sorry I was that I had neglected his needs in the midst of trying to serve our family. My intentions were good. I just lost sight of the priorities. This also led me to analyze my own sexual needs and how we could better fulfill each other. He was not demanding in any way, but our love for each other created a new awareness in this area of our relationship. I made a decision and told him what I wanted to do.

"I want to make a commitment to you that from now on we will make love anytime you want to, and whenever you feel any temptation, come to me before acting on it! I want to fulfill you." He was elated that I would be willing to make that kind of commitment to him and was more excited about me than I had seen him in a long time. In fact, he was so excited, he laughingly told me, "I want to take out an ad in the newspaper and tell the whole world!" (I guess I just did.)

The fun part is that as I tried to live up to my commitment and serve him, he actually started to serve me even more. He got to the place where he was so sensitive to meeting my needs sexually and understanding of my day and pressures with the children, he would do household work, take care of the baby in the night, and many other things to show his love and consideration for me. I didn't use the lovemaking to get this. I gave it freely and enjoyed doing so, and in return he demonstrated his love in many other ways as well.

> No act can be quite so intimate as the sexual embrace. In its accomplishment, for all who have reached a reasonably human degree of development, the communion of bodies becomes the communion of souls.
> HAVELOCK ELLIS

During the first Marriage Makeover conference we hosted, Gary and I separated the men from the women, and we each shared our perspective on sex. To our surprise, every man in the conference admitted to private temptations and battles with pornography and second glances at women with whom they thought of a sexual encounter. Many of these marriages were moving toward possible destruction.

I shared with the women about Gary's confession to me and how we had become even greater friends and lovers. I challenged them to treat their husbands with the same forgiveness and understanding they would a friend who was struggling in some area. We would be quick to offer them God's forgiveness and extend our hand in support to help them through a tough trial or problem. So why wouldn't we give our husbands the same support and consideration?

In the next session, men readily asked for their wives' forgiveness. Women all over the room returned the humility and honesty with reassurance and renewed love. The confession brought healing and restoration. I have never forgotten the sight of tears flowing down faces all over the room and couples holding each other in a never-let-you-go embrace. Several rocked their partners back and forth and cried as they held them. When they renewed their vows, they did so with a deeper understanding of real commitment.

Within Marriage, Sex Is Holy

I was only able to share this healing with other couples because I had walked through my own restoration in this area. After overcoming years of guilt and misunderstandings about sex, I understood that God designed our bodies to give both men and women intense pleasure, physically and emotionally. This is not an act to please men alone, which was another wrong thought process I adopted from the strong anti-male messages I heard as a young woman. "Men are just out to use women. All they want is sex." Television series during the 1970s, such as *The Golddiggers*, portrayed women as sex symbols and gave me a warped view of men and sex in general. I rebelled intensely against the nonsensical displays of women in glittery gold hot pants dancing in cages, and rightfully so! But once I came into God's Kingdom, I saw sex from a new perspective. I began to see the beauty, the mutual enjoyment that was intended by our Creator, and the oneness a couple could experience as they committed to fidelity and sought to please each other sexually rather than misuse sex.

As I understood more about God's view of sex, I was able to enjoy lovemaking without feeling used, ashamed, or cheated. I also learned about my own body, and that it was God who created the clitoris (and Adam probably named it) and gave women the physical features to enjoy sex. This tiny organ by which a woman can experience a climax or orgasm has no other purpose except for sheer personal enjoyment. I learned that sexual intimacy was created by God and is therefore a spiritual act.

Genesis 2:25 illustrates this, speaking of the first man and woman, "*The man and his wife were both naked, and they felt no shame.*" This was before the command to bear children, so their sexual union was not just about procreation, but was also about mutual pleasure and oneness. To view sex as a means to create children only is short-sighted and removes the beauty of oneness that a husband and wife experience in intercourse. There is also a beautiful allegory between the marriage of a husband and wife and Christ and His covenant with us.

Sexual intimacy parallels the blood covenant established by Christ in the New Covenant where He gives Himself for us. A woman typically sheds blood as her hymen is penetrated for the first time in intercourse. This mirrors the blood covenant God made with man, as His Son shed His blood in a covenant relationship with us. When a husband and wife share this experience, they have not only entered into a covenant by vow during the marriage ceremony, they are also entering into a sacred blood covenant through sexual intercourse. We use the phrase "consummating the marriage." To consummate is the act of officially carrying out the spoken commitment—the seal of a lifetime covenant relationship. A blood covenant symbolizes that everything I am and possess belongs to my husband, including my body, and he belongs to me in the same fashion. Each spouse is making this commitment before God, and the marriage bed is holy, pure, and undefiled (see Heb. 13:4). Within marriage, sex is not just right, it is holy.

We find our greatest fulfillment in becoming one—in both possessing and serving our beloved. The earth-cursed system has it all wrong. The world says sex is about taking for physical and physiological relief only, but we can never be satisfied if it is all about us. They miss the point by separating love and sex. In God's design, love multiplies and emotions of love increase as we give of ourselves to each other, both in commitment and sexual intimacy within the marriage.

We love what we invest into. As we share ourselves intimately, we lose ourselves in pleasing our mate, and the investment strengthens our love. Our bodies are not our own, but rather we have pledged them to our mate as an expression of our love and devotion.

> Human sexuality is too noble and beautiful a thing, too profound a form of experience, to turn into a mere technique of physical relief or a foolish and irrelevant pastime.
>
> J.V.L. CASSERLEY

The apostle Paul couldn't be much more specific regarding sex within marriage: *"The husband should fulfill his marital duty to his wife, and likewise the wife to her husband. The wife's body does not belong to her alone but also to her husband. In the same way, the husband's body does not belong to him alone but also to his wife. Do not deprive each other except by mutual consent and for a time, so that you may devote yourselves to prayer. Then come together again so that Satan will not tempt you because of your lack of self-control"* (1 Cor. 7:3–5).

Everywhere we turn, blatant sexual messages scream at us from every media outlet, yet 20 percent of relationships in America are reportedly sexless. In other words, sexual relationship occurs ten or less times in a given year. With so much propaganda and open attitudes toward sex, why does it seem that more people are less satisfied with their lives in this area? Other reports confirm that people in a marriage relationship are the most satisfied with their sex lives.

I believe that anytime we make an idol of something and use it outside of the context of love, it leaves us empty and wanting for more. Lust is never fulfilled. There is a difference between demanding what we want in bed and giving ourselves to our mate to please him. If both persons are trying to please each other, then sex the way it was intended for mutual pleasure can exist and thrive in the marriage.

Igniting Passion

After the prerequisite of marriage as a basis for "right" sexual relationship, we need to learn to understand the differences between men and women and how to please our spouse. I want to share some of the differences I have learned through experience. Men are almost always stimulated by sight, whereas women tend to be moved by emotional feelings before sexual arousal occurs. For a man, sex can be an event and not necessarily connected to other events of the day. Whereas, we women see sex as an extension of our relationship, and every part of the relationship—the good, bad, or ugly—enters into the bedroom. I have heard it said that a man could probably have sex while he was having a heated argument with his wife! Not so for us ladies. We are focused on every aspect of the relationship, much like a satellite dish that pulls in and processes every television signal. Communication, words, touches, tenderness, consideration, the kids, and privacy all play into our ability to relax and enjoy our partner. With that in mind, we need to communicate our desires to our husband and make allowance for sex in our schedule and plans.

One wife told me, "We just don't have time for sex." I asked her whether she had time to take her children to school, get her hair cut, and even to clean the house. She said yes, but no time for sex. The bottom line is: Whatever we esteem as a priority, we make time for in our lives. Sexual intimacy has to be a major priority in our marriages if we want them to last and remain faithful as the apostle Paul stated about not letting ourselves be tempted because we fail to fulfill our "marital duty."

Now, I don't know about you, but I don't like the word "duty." It sounds like…a duty. The word that would better describe this is our "act of serving." No man wants to make love to a "duty-bound dead fish" for a wife. It's important to a man to know he is wanted and what he has to give to his wife is one of her greatest desires. He wants her to occasionally be the initiator of sex and seduce him.

How do you seduce your husband? Yes, it is fine to seduce your husband as long as your intent is purely for your mutual enjoyment and not to manipulate him for some other favor. Proverbs 7:21 unveils how an illicit woman seduces a man: "*With her enticing speech she caused him to yield, with her flattering lips she seduced him*" (NKJV). Another version mentions "her smooth talk." Married women should learn a few things that keep their husbands coming to them instead. After all, why do men pay for phone sex if there is not something exciting to a man about a woman talking to him in a sexy way about wanting him and what she wants to do with him? Proverbs 7 also mentions her racy attire, which is not appropriate for public, but certainly fine for the privacy of the bedroom! These are two keys to ignite a man's passion—use them well.

The Song of Solomon

I laugh at how so many magazines promise new moves and secrets to sex. They are right in the Bible! You don't believe me? Have you ever read the Song of Solomon? This is an entire book about sex and passion within a marriage. Now if you read it in the King James Version, you may get a little lost, but if you unfold its mysteries in a more modern version, you find a whole lotta passion going on.

The Song of Solomon describes a couple's wedding night with great detail and even their romance as it unfolds through time. She speaks of her old and new ways to please her man. We should always be exploring new ways to keep our sexual intimacy alive with our husband. Women can get prudish and distant over time, and men can get mechanical, like a football player with only one move in the playbook, but we should both attempt to stay fresh and experience greater fulfillment as our love deepens. And keep in mind that laughter goes a long way. We need to be relaxed and just have fun in the bedroom. You can choose to get bent out of shape if things don't go your way, or you can choose to laugh at the situation. Laughter is more enjoyable.

> Rowing in Eden—
> Ah, the Sea!
> Might I but moor—
> Tonight—
> In Thee!
>
> EMILY DICKINSON

Take time to care for your health, your body, and your appearance. Since men are stimulated by sight, we should accentuate the positive. Every woman has positive traits. The right clothing or lingerie, makeup, fitness, and effort can make any woman more attractive to her lover. But honestly, the most attractive trait of a woman is her respect and desire toward her man. I have never forgotten hearing a preacher tell the women in his church to throw out their "holey" panties. He wasn't talking about "holy," but rather those with holes in them. I couldn't help but look at his wife and wonder if he was sending her a signal.

The Song of Solomon records a very romantic account of sexual intimacy, some of which, because we have lost the cultural understanding, may be laughable; however, the principles remain true. In chapter 4 the lover details every part of his beloved's body, including her eyes, hair, teeth, lips, mouth, temples, neck, and breasts, using picturesque metaphors. He speaks of her beauty and her kisses and her scent that are so pleasing to him. Then he ends by paralleling her vagina with a locked-up garden, a spring enclosed. He continues by describing her as a fountain of gardens, with choice fruits, incenses, and finest of spices, a well of living gardens.

She responds by telling him to awake and come "blow on" her garden, that its fragrances may spread abroad. "*Let my lover come into his garden and taste its choice fruits*" (v. 16). The lover responds, "*I have come into my garden, my sister, my bride; I have gathered my myrrh with my spice. I have eaten my honeycomb and my honey; I have drunk my wine and my milk*" (5:1). Clearly, things get off to a great start in their marriage, and their love progresses over time.

However, as chapter 5 continues, the lover comes again for more intimacy with her as she slept (5:2). This scene is typical of how we ladies can get a man, and he thinks that sex will be available to him 24/7, but once married we turn him away. Her lover, her husband, knocks at her door wanting to have more, but she actually says, "*I'm in my nightgown—do you expect me to get dressed? I'm bathed and in bed—do you want me to get dirty?*"

(5:3 MSG). By the time she gets up and goes to him, he has already left. The story goes on that she looks through the night to find him, but the city night watchmen beat her up as she searches to find his love again, and she finally finds him back at his workplace. In some ways, situations in life can sort of beat us up if we lose the intimate connection with our husband, and he will typically resort to working more hours to release his frustration.

Once together again, she describes that she is faint with love for her lover, and in chapter 6 he tells her of her beauty, body part by part, but this time he uses new adjectives and comparisons. In chapter 7, she says, "*Come, my lover, let us go to the country-side, let us spend the night in the villages. Let us go early to the vineyards to see if the vines have budded, if their blossoms have opened, and if the pomegranates are in bloom—there I will give you my love*" (vv. 11–12). In verse 13, she offers him "mandrakes," which were considered an aphrodisiac. She tells him that at their "door is every delicacy, both new and old, that I have stored up for you, my lover." Wow! Here's a woman basically saying, "Let's go to a hotel and feast on each other. I have some new ways to make love with you, and I am high with ecstasy for you, and I intend to make you the same way!"

Many times Gary and I have felt like the circumstances or pressures of life were pulling us away from each other. We have often initiated going away for a vacation or even the night away from the kids, housework, ministry, and business. Sometimes we have even done this on a whim.

With five children, our house can be like Grand Central Station. One night, after one delay and then another to be alone, I told Gary, "Grab a toothbrush, and let's get out of here!" We drove to a nice inn not too far from our house. Entering the lobby, we asked for a room. The female clerk, noticing we had no luggage and that Gary's toothbrush was sticking out of his pocket, looked at me with disgust. I think she believed I was "the other woman," having a rendezvous with a married man. She told us in a snide way, "We have no rooms," despite the fact that the parking lot was almost empty! *How could they have no rooms?* I thought. I started to put up an argument and tell her we had been married 25 years, but instead we left, giggling as we got into our car and drove to another inn just down the road. This time the toothbrush was tucked away, and we were successful getting our suite. It was just what we needed—sleeping in, eating a quiet breakfast, and then returning to the world. We have learned that we need time alone. Nothing can build relationship like getting some down time just to make love and care for each other away from the pressures we all encounter.

The entire discourse from the female lover in chapter 8 of the Song of Solomon ends with her saying that in his eyes, she has become one who brings contentment to him, and that her vineyard is hers to give (see vv. 10–12). Sexual intimacy is ours to give, and when we choose to share it with our lifetime lover, it is very satisfying and develops an intimacy that one-night stands can never offer. We will all be tempted at times with potentially illicit opportunities outside of our marriage, but when we recognize the trouble it will bring to our marriage relationship, it can never be worth it. I have spoken with women and men who regret making mistakes in this area, and although forgiveness and restoration are possible, trust takes a long time to rebuild, especially in us emotionally based females.

The Message Bible reads, "*Sexual drives are strong, but marriage is strong enough to contain them and provide for a balanced and fulfilling sexual life in a world of sexual disorder"* (1 Cor. 7:3).

There is an old saying that the devil tries everything he can do to get us in bed before we get married, and everything he can do to keep us out of it once we are married. Don't ever let that happen.

The woman who has "IT" guards the precious gift of sexuality and only shares it in the beautiful commitment of marriage.

get Family Relations right:

LIFE'S GREATEST GIFTS LIE HERE

6 get Family Relations right:

LIFE'S GREATEST GIFTS LIE HERE

A hundred years from now, it will not matter
what my bank account was, the sort of
house I lived in, or the kind of car I drove.
But the world may be different because
I was important in the life of a child.

Forest E. Witcraft

O f all the rewards I have enjoyed in life, our children are the most.
Looking back over the years, I never think I missed great
opportunities because I chose to be at home with them, and I
cannot think of any more worthwhile investment with higher
dividends. Occasionally, I got distracted with other pursuits,
and at one point I almost gave up my stay-at-home mom decision for what appeared to be a lucrative career, but God always
managed to bring me back to the main focus of our marriage

and children before any trouble ensued. Proverbs 11:29 (NKJV) states, "*He who troubles his own house will inherit the wind,*" which is not a pleasant picture. We "trouble" our home when we undervalue family relationships by treating our family as disposable and our loved ones with neglect and disrespect. Selfishness and self-preservation are the motivating forces behind this trouble.

As a young woman growing up in a culture that promoted the exchange of the role of wife and mother for the "glories" of a career and travel, I never planned to be married or to have children. While some childhood friends played house with their dolls and pretended they would some day marry and set up house, I left those fantasies behind at an early age and began to dream of careers, first as a teacher. I drew pictures of myself as a schoolteacher (hair in a bun and all!). After school, I would set up the "neighborhood classroom" in the basement of a friend, where I tutored many of the local kids who were struggling with various subjects.

By the time I was in fifth grade, I envisioned myself as the first female president of the United States, and I was determined that the concept of a "family" would not interfere with my plans. Therein lies the struggle that many women in our world face today. As women, we're told we can "have it all" and not lose or exchange anything, but I cannot think of a loss greater than not experiencing motherhood or missing it by being too preoccupied to actually mother my children. To nurture a child and secure them in my arms, to get up in the middle of the night to comfort, console, and love selflessly is and has been the most fulfilling experience of my life. The love I share with my husband is incredible and sacred, but the responsibility and privilege of completely molding the life of a tiny innocent one who is looking to me with trust have impacted me like no other.

According to my former world viewpoint, when my pastor taught the message "It's a High Calling to Bear Godly Seed," this would have been a chauvinistic message that narrowed the role of a woman to that of a baby production center. But rather than strike a chord of disgust or anger in me, that message went straight to my heart. He read the Scripture that states that God made a husband and wife one *"because he was seeking a godly offspring [seed]"* (Mal. 2:15). Throughout his message, he reinforced the beauty and "holy work" of raising godly children for the Lord. No longer did this sound like a "rip-off" or a prison sentence for women, but for the first time I saw motherhood as a calling and an honor from God that would one day become the center of my focus and life and bring me the greatest joy as I shared this with the man I "needed" most.

> Our greatest danger in life is in permitting the urgent things to crowd out the important.
> CHARLES E. HUMMEL

After meeting and marrying my husband in the ensuing years, our first child came, and I began to learn just how much joy and satisfaction come from the hard work raising children can bring! I recommend it as the best "self-improvement" course you can take, if you do it with the right heart, attitude, and commitment. Very few experiences have caused me to change more as a person, and I know I am a "better individual" for nurturing children.

The Importance of Strong Families

There are principles for building a strong family, just as there are for building a solid marriage, and it all starts with God's original creation. God is love, and in His love He wanted a family, and from that desire He envisioned each of us, His unique children. It's a beautiful picture that the God of the universe, Creator of everything, wanted more than to make vast space, planets, trees, and animals. What God really wanted was a family, and He actually made the other parts of His creation for our enjoyment.

I have learned more about the heart of God and His love from my experience with parenting than any other endeavor. People are eternal and infinitely more important than all the other components of creation. I have met some of the most accomplished women in the world, and yet they still seem to communicate more about their families or their longing for a family than anything else. After all, nothing we accomplish in life or become has full expression without the ability to share and pass our accomplishments along to others. My point is that in spite of all our accomplishments as women, our deepest inner desire is for family.

We live in a world that talks a lot about our family choices—pro-choice, planned parenting, limited family size, and new definitions of what a family consists. Regardless of how we "engineer family," we can never get away from God's established design and have lasting success. Unfortunately, wrongdoing has corrupted the original plan, but instead of returning to the truths of God's plan, many people are trying to redefine family. I understand there has been pain and brokenness in this area, but we can never get back on track with redefinitions. We need to return to and reinstate the eternal truths of God's design if family is to survive.

Belonging to a functional family is such a vital part of life and our society. Families are support systems that should offer children a foundation for living and provide information, encouragement, and training. Most important, they can either create loving security in which children can thrive or break children's hearts with pain and separation. Once broken, it is sad to watch the spiral effect on children's lives as they grow up physically but remain broken on the inside. Gangs, crime, domestic violence, murder, drugs, pornography, alcohol and other addictions, sexual deviancy, severe depression, and mental disorders are growing by skyrocketing numbers, and they can be traced back largely to problematic childhoods and the breakdown of the family. History confirms that whenever

> A child's life is like a piece of paper on which every person leaves a mark.
> CHINESE PROVERB

the family unit is broken down, and there is no longer a commitment to the development and protection of family, a nation eventually self-destructs or falls into anarchy.

Children, unfortunately, become the victims of the worst that society offers, and what is written on a tender child's heart always has a lasting impression. Jesus said, *"And if anyone causes one of these little ones who believe in me to sin, it would be better for him to be thrown into the sea with a large millstone tied around his neck"* (Mark 9:42).

A Lifelong Commitment With Fabulous Rewards

I would not be honest with you if I made motherhood sound as a glorious, easy endeavor, with no strings attached. Becoming a mother means that our children are "attached" to us throughout our lives, just in differing ways at different times. It is a lifelong commitment that has seasons of investment as well as reward—more reward than sacrifice by far.

When children are newborns, we are their complete source of nourishment, emotionally and physically (especially if you're breastfeeding) and spiritually. That little child is looking almost solely to us for everything he or she needs. This can be an overwhelming feeling, since most of us tend to enter mother-hood somewhat, if not very, selfish in our outlook.

Especially when children are small, the physical demands can be very exhausting. Prayer got me through many moments of stress or self-denial. A few times, I remember rocking a crying baby while I cried with them. Potty training seemed to be one of the bigger hurdles for me! When I would hit a wall and feel like I couldn't give of myself one more minute, which happened often, I tried to always remind myself, "This too shall pass." There were times I felt as though I wasn't going to make it or wished I could escape and run away and "do something important and glamor-ous," but instead I would pray for help. I cannot imagine what I would have lost had I opted out for what would have been only moments of temporal pleasures. The temptation to escape from pressure is always there, at some times more than others, but it's sticking to the commitment when we don't always see the out-come that makes it worthwhile.

However, lest you think I had it easy, this one story should con-vince you that was not the case. It began when my daughter, Amy, needed a dress to wear the next day for a church produc-tion—not just any dress; no, it had to be *red, black*, and *white*. At the time, I had three children—the first two were lively, but the third, well, lively didn't do justice to describe him. He was so full of bounce and life (thankfully as I reflect now) that he could turn any day into an adventure…or worse. (I think he gets some, if not much, of that from me!)

After a day of shopping with the three little kids, I was tired and didn't know where I was going to find this "dress" for the next morning. We had closed down every store in our area except the

24-hour "buy-everything-here" store located in a tough part of town. It was already 11 P.M., and I was desperate. I was certain my husband was wondering where we were at this late hour. I was uncomfortable with the store's surroundings and the people who shopped this late at night, but this was my last chance.

As I headed for the girls' department, I remembered that the dog needed food, so we veered off to the grocery section, where I threw a 50-pound bag of dog food on the bottom rack of my now full cart, kids in tow noisily playing around and on the cart. Unfortunately, the bag caught the edge of one of the cart's wheels and burst open, shooting dog food onto the floor. I instructed Amy, the oldest, to wait with the other two while I found help to clean up the mess. When I returned quickly with the late-night department manager, much to my shock and embarrassment, I found my lively three-year-old son running and sliding in the dog food, little balls of dog food scattered all up and down the aisle of the store. It was unbelievable how far it had traveled and multiplied. He was having the time of his life!

People were standing all around and watching him. I was mortified, and after many apologies, we scurried off to the girls' department, where I found a black and white checked dress with a red sash! Just what we needed. So now with two carts full of merchandise and three children, I came and waited in an excruciatingly long line to check out. *What were so many people doing out this late?* I wondered. Then I began to realize people were looking at us the same way! *What were a mother and her three children doing out after midnight?*

As we went to leave the store, Amy tried to control the youngest child while I pushed a cart and little Tim pushed a second cart behind me. The next thing I knew, my head hit the floor with a thump and all I saw was stars. Tim had hit me in the heels with his cart and knocked me flat on my back! I was lying on the floor, everything went totally silent in the store checkout line, and I had to shake myself to remember where I was as I slowly sat up. All eyes were on me as a clerk beckoned, "Ma'am, are you all right?" Tim began to cry, and I thought I might. We managed to recover and head out of the store.

Given the dark parking lot and strange late-night shoppers, I tried to hurry to load my children and groceries and make my getaway. I gave a strong push to one of the carts, motioning my son to grab it, but he was distracted with the other cart while my cart hurled across the lot. I took off running and caught it before it hit a parked car. Exhausted and disgusted, we left the parking lot and fifteen minutes later pulled into the drive of our farmhouse.

> There are two lasting bequests we can give our children: one is roots, the other is wings.
> HODDING CARTER

These were pre-cell-phone days. I was certain my husband was worried sick about where we were. Instead, I found the door was locked, and I had no key with me. I rang the bell. I beat on the door. I continued to do so for what seemed like an eternity, and finally a sleepy-headed Gary emerged at the door. Peering out into the dark, he said groggily, "Who is it?" "Your wife and three children!" I yelled back with the feisty spirit my husband knows too well. He had fallen asleep waiting and completely forgotten we weren't home!

We survived…and even thrived. And so will you!

By the way, our boisterous third born has become an excellent drummer and musician, and he is very evangelistic. He needs the personality and energy God gave Him to be who he is today, and I am very proud of him. Our youngest child, by way of contrast, has just enough of the wit of her older brothers and sisters, with a touch of humorous sarcasm and sweetness. We need her to bring our feet back to the ground and laugh when we all get overly ambitious in our family.

Every child is gifted uniquely and has his or her own special personality with strengths and weaknesses. We need to celebrate the differences of our children and not compare them to one another. God has a plan for the way He made them. Learn to work with your children's personalities and especially coach them in the areas of their weakness, but never make them feel they are less than others because of differences. We are all an accumulation of God's giftedness mixed with the order of our birth and the environment we have developed within. None of this takes God by surprise. He can use it all!

Raising Healthy, Well-Adjusted Kids

The rewards of working together, playing together, and celebrating together as a family are greater than the offerings of any corporate boardroom, and "the hand that rocks the cradle" truly does rule the world. I am convinced this is why the enemy seeks to divide the family. If God made a husband and wife one because He sought a godly seed, I believe the enemy tries to divide them into two separate, self-serving individuals because he seeks the seed as well.

If moms and dads are too worried about themselves and miss the big picture, the division that happens between them opens the children up to attacks from the enemy. You cannot have whole and happy children without a whole and happy marriage. For instance, if we put our children as a priority over our husband, this is a serious mistake. It models for children that they are in control and sets them up to be manipulative. As soon as they figure out that Mom will do whatever they want, they begin to pit Mom against Dad to get their way, and the division locks in.

Children are very smart. It's human nature (I should say the "sin nature") that we are all born with that makes us discover and uncover ways to get what we want when we want it. Children are no different in this. They may be innocent in many ways, but they quickly learn how to play the same games they see their parents play in order to get their way.

This is why in order to be good parents we must be willing to learn and grow into men and women who do things the way God instructs. This is a process. The Word of God has to be the standard in our lives if we are going to be the right model for our children to follow. Jesus must be our example, and our lives must be lives that model faith in every way. From the time our children are young, we must give them the security of our love as well as the knowledge that there is One who loves them more than we do—our heavenly Father. They must learn of His love, and we must refer to His ways and Word as the foundation for every decision we make.

Faith isn't as much taught as it is caught. Be the right example for your children. Pray over them while you carry them to birth and for the rest of their lives. Show them as small toddlers how to praise the Lord and raise their little hands to God. Hug the Bible and tell them it is God's Word, a letter of love to us. Teach them how to share. The first words I said to our little ones were "Jesus loves you," "Jesus says to share," "Jesus says to love," "Jesus says to forgive," and "We love Jesus." If we all practiced these simple truths, there would be very little else we needed in life.

From the time our children could move, they were praising the Lord. We not only went as a family to church, but we talked of God's Word to them consistently. We read books about Jesus. We listened to and praised God with the music in our home. I don't regret that in the earlier days we often didn't have a working television in our home. It required us to talk, play, create forts with blankets, play in the sandbox, walk to the park, and tell stories to one another. (Our daughter Polly always wanted to tell me a story instead of me telling her one!) I wrote Scriptures on cards and put them on mirrors and the refrigerator. If they struggled, I found a Scripture to give them direction and answers. This is "training" them up in the way they should go, and as they grow older, they will not depart from it (see Prov. 22:6).

Part of this training is making sure the educational choices we make for them are not just providing "teaching" but training. We chose to home-educate our children for this reason. As I examined the other choices, the public system did not give them the training or education I felt they needed, and the private choices, although many of them were Christian in commitment, still had many downfalls. I home-educated our first child until the third grade and then intended to enter her into a private school. After she was tested, the principal said, "Just between you and me, your daughter is well-above her grade in scores, and she seems so well-adjusted, happy, and well-behaved. Why do you want to enroll her here?" I laughed and said, "That's what I thought I was supposed to do." He said, "Whatever you're doing, it's working. I would continue." I walked out and continued to train all of our children at home through high school.

They have all done exceptionally well in college and are happy young adults. I often have people ask me how they have such wonderful social skills. I think because they were home-educated, and since they were not kept from having other positive growing experiences, they have a strong moral compass and self-worth, not based on peer pressure. I made the commitment to guide their education, while also surrounding them with many opportunities to grow and be exposed to travel, museums, and church activities, such as drama, puppet ministry, music, public speaking, and more. The funds we saved on private education gave us opportunities to travel across Europe, go on mission trips, explore America and almost all the national parks, as well as remote destinations such as Corsica. We have had an amazing family journey.

Our children are also best of friends for all the experiences we have had together. When the children were small, I would read them books and show them distant places, saying, "One day I will take you to these places and show them to you myself." On a tight budget, we started our travels by loading up in an old van with camping gear and camping in a national forest in Colorado. Hiking deep into the woods with our gear in tow, we set up our first camp just before dusk and made campfire foil dinners. But as we were all falling asleep, lying shoulder-to-shoulder in our sleeping bags, my husband suddenly jumped to his feet and started hitting the side of the tent and yelling, "Get away! Get!" We had no idea what was going on! We laughed as we realized he might have been dreaming. He said he heard something outside, which left us all thinking bears or mountain lions. As we once again began to dose off, I began to dream we were surrounded by bears, then I let out a blood-curdling scream, scaring the entire family. We laughed as we realized there was no reason to be frightened.

Later, Amy told me she was fine until both of us scared her with our panic, and then she lay awake the rest of the night.

We decided the next night to sleep next to a rushing river, crisp and clean. We placed a well-lit lantern outside the tent so we would be able to see any predators that might venture near. All settled in, seven sleepyheads side-by-side in our tent, we suddenly froze when we saw a giant shadow on the inside of the tent wall. My husband eased out of the sleeping bag and carefully maneuvered around the bodies on the tent floor. With an ax in hand, he unzipped the tent, ready to attack. To our astonishment, a chipmunk had climbed up the tent pole, and with the lantern's projection its shadow seemed like a huge animal. We laughed for hours and told jokes, poking one another and pretending to hear something.

Many camping trips later, we had traveled most of the United States, even Alaska, renting an RV and traveling through the rugged wilderness. Our finances began to increase, and when Amy was graduating from college, she said, "Mom, if you're ever going to take us to Europe like you used to tell us, we should do it now." She and I planned the entire four-week trip abroad, and I could fill another book with stories, fun, and adventures we experienced.

> The greatest gifts my parents gave to me... were their unconditional love and set of values. Values that they lived and didn't just lecture about. Values that included an understanding of the simple difference between right and wrong, a belief in God, the importance of hard work and education, self-respect and a belief in America.
>
> COLIN POWELL

A few years later, as I led the youth ministry of our church, we took 36 young people with adult leaders to minister in Albania. I marveled as I watched not only my children, but an entire group of amazing young people, minister in orphanages, city-wide meetings, and a youth meeting in the main city of Tirana. They shared the love of God, cleaned town streets, sang, danced, acted in dramas, cared for children, and prayed for many. I feel as though our choices not only affected our children in a positive way, but gave us an opportunity to do something to affect others' lives, too.

All of these opportunities gave our children and me rich experiences, memories for a lifetime. With three of my children having weddings in 13 months and a fourth child purchasing a home, as my children leave the nest, I am the most grateful, fulfilled mother in the world. I was there. I didn't miss a beat, and I don't regret the investment of time, love, and labor. It has been the greatest fun I could ever want. Part of me wishes it could go on forever, but I am so glad to know they are starting a whole new adventure with their own beautiful families. It just keeps getting better. I look forward to grandchildren too!

Training Is More Important Than Teaching

I like to think in many ways our family "bucked the system" and explored new ways to live life—free and together. I know that our choices may sound radical to some, but I believe God intended us to squeeze every minute of enjoyment out of life. Our children were trained for life by truly living every day with us, helping us run our business, conducting ministry, and watching us handle life's situations. In my opinion, what better training could we offer? Regardless of the choices you make in educating your children, recognize that you are the one who has the responsibility to lead, guide, and direct them. The school system, the church, or others are tools, but you must be the main source of their training.

Training is so much more important than teaching. Training models for them what they "are" to do; teaching says this is what they "should" do. It is easier to follow when it is demonstrated. You can "say" what you like, but your children will "do" what they see you do. If you are critical and put down others, so will your children. If you yell, so will they. If you show disrespect for authority, your husband, or God's representatives, so will they. Our children replicate what we are. Become the person God intended you to be and humbly ask forgiveness when you are wrong. Children also need to see humility modeled. Too many parents can hide behind pride and refuse to let their children know that we all make mistakes, but no one is ever too big to say, "I'm sorry. I was wrong." In this way, God trains us as we train our children.

We have always required our children to admit their errors and take responsibility by apologizing and, when needed, making restitution (fixing what they did wrong if appropriate). Then the other child or person they mistreated was instructed to say, "I forgive you," and we asked them to hug each other. Very simply, they are modeling love, acceptance, and forgiveness, and also taking personal responsibility for their wrong acts. How many marriages and homes would be more peaceful if the words "I'm sorry" and "I forgive you" were spoken more frequently? The hug makes both the offender and the offended make a decision to choose the way of love.

I tried very hard to not raise my voice or yell at anyone in the course of correction. This shows respect for them and others. Even when someone has done something seriously wrong, to shout or demean them is to make them feel belittled and dis-respected. If this is the method of communication you demonstrate for your children, this will be the method that they communicate back to you and eventually their own families. It also adds to an already difficult situation, creating isolation and anger when personal responsibility, repentance, forgiveness, and acceptance are what everyone involved really needs and desires. There is a time to be firm to convey the seriousness of an offense, but not in a demeaning manner.

On occasion, there are times when we "blow it" as parents and need to admit that the way we handled the situation was not the best and ask for forgiveness of our children for the way in which we reacted. Just because the child did something wrong doesn't mean that our response in an ungodly way is justified. However, don't let the child use your outburst or improper behavior to manipulate you away from dealing with the issue of their behavior or attitude. Accept your responsibility for handling it wrong, apologize, and then move quickly on to dealing with their behavior. Children can be masterful at distracting us with our own issues in order to keep the focus off of their misbehavior.

> At every step the child should be allowed to meet the real experiences of life; the thorns should never be plucked from his roses.
>
> ELLEN KEY

Discipline That Corrects Problems

Although much of our culture has rejected the concept of personal responsibility and consequences for wrong behavior, I believe another key ingredient in training children is to discipline them so that the offensive behavior is not repeated over and over and becomes a lifetime habit. The concept of discipline is very clear in the Word of God, and if we want and expect the results of God's blessing on our family, we must choose to do it His way. Any other method will prove to be independent of His counsel and will not produce the desired results. If we rebel against God's system of disciplining our children, how can we not expect our children to rebel against us? If we reject the clear instructions to discipline our children as stated in Scripture, we are rejecting the God of those instructions. To do so means we will be unsuccessful at child training.

"Discipline your son while there is hope, but do not [indulge your angry resentments by undue chastisements and] set yourself to his ruin" (Prov. 19:18 AMP). Examples of undue chastisements are to discipline for childish accidents or out of resentment because you are under pressure and they require your attention or have needs. Some parents will also not take the time to discipline, because they are too caught up in their own wants or requirements. This is a serious error. The seed you refuse to pluck from the ground today will grow up into a tree tomorrow. It is much easier to deal with behavior when it is small and has not become a serious habit than to wait.

I have seen children make excuses and lie to their parents about situations, and the parent makes excuses for the child, believing them over and over, when teachers, relatives, and friends have shared with them what the child is actually doing. I watch these children grow into teenage liars who know no other way to handle their errors. Instead of admitting their mistakes, willful sins, and behavior, they learn to cover it and live with the full guilt and condemnation. *"All wrongdoing is sin"* (1 John 5:17). Yes, *sin.* It may not be a popular twenty-first-century word, but it is still as alive as it was when Adam and Eve disobeyed and invited it as a curse on all their offspring.

We discipline our children to separate them from sin. What we are saying to them is, "You are my child, and I believe in you, and because I believe in you and the future God has for you, I must separate this sin or 'situation' from you by disciplining you. This will help you, and I do this because I love you too much to leave you this way. I am taking the time to instruct you and to help you to remember to not do this again." The instruction will be received if the discipline has made them truly repentant. A repentant heart is a heart that doesn't want to make the same decision next time and that welcomes correction in order to grow and change. Many adults do not have teachable hearts because they were not disciplined correctly as children, so they have either become irresponsible from lack of correction or hardened by discipline that was not given with a spirit of love.

Considering discipline, some parents discipline in a harsh manner, while others neglect to discipline at all. The motive for correct discipline is to help children take responsibility, admit their mistakes, receive forgiveness, and restoration. Instead, some parents take a harsh legalistic stance and want the child to feel shamed, shunned, and ashamed. Shame is not a good feeling and makes a child feel worthless. These parents use shame as a means to control their child's behavior and put them in a prison of guilt. Inevitably, when this child eventually rebels against them, they heap more shame on the child and act as though they are totally innocent of their child's behavior. Often religious parents demean their kids to others in order to cover their own guilty hands and quote Scriptures out of context to make it seem as though parents have no control over their children's upbringing or choices.

Do not discipline children for making a mistake, such as accidentally spilling a drink or dropping and breaking something, getting on your nerves, or having a toilet training accident. Never call them names or give them negative labels. In essence, when you do so, you are cursing them with your words, and they will hear those words replayed over and over throughout their lives in moments when they need confidence instead of condemnation. No words have power over our lives as do the words of our parents, with one exception—the Word of God that brings healing to the wounded souls of adults who were berated with harshness as a child.

A child should be disciplined for willful misbehavior or outright rebellion. Ask yourself, "Is this misbehavior or rebellion or was this simply an accident?" Be honest. We can all make excuses for behavior, but excuses don't usually count in court, so don't make them! Little Johnny was tired, so he pitched a fit in the floor. Susie was hungry, so she bit Sally. Terry was angry, so she broke mommy's vase. Joey wanted the toy, so he hit his sister to get it. The list of excuses goes on and on. Don't go there. Is it misbehavior or not? Or, better said, "Is it behavior you want to remain or be separated (cut off) from their life? Will you be pleased if they're still doing it as an adult?" If not, you better deal with it while they're two or five or seven!

> Call them rules or call them limits, good ones, I believe, have this in common: they serve reasonable purposes; they are practical and within a child's capability; they are consistent; and they are an expression of loving concern.
>
> **FRED ROGERS**

Don't laugh off a child's disobedience and say, "Isn't she cute!" as she pouts and hits the dog when she's two years old. You are training her that her behavior is acceptable now, so it becomes a habit later. Occasionally, I have had to almost turn my head to keep our children from seeing me laugh at a behavior that is really funny when they're so little, but I don't dare let them see me laugh and reinforce this behavior as a way to make mommy "happy." Trust me, it won't be funny when they grow up!

Administering Discipline

Our children need to always know that we believe them, trust them, love them over anybody else, other than our spouse, but this shouldn't lead to our blind acceptance of excuses they make for their behavior. As parents, we can refuse to believe that our "little darling" did anything wrong, and some kids can put on Academy Award-winning performances to prove their innocence. We need to listen to the sound advice and counsel of those we trust around us in order to sometimes see clearly that our child is being dishonest or "pulling the wool over our eyes." Don't get offended if someone who has a committed heart toward you shares a behavior or concern with you about your child in a private manner. Pray and ask the Lord to show you the reality and look hard and honestly at the truth. Usually, most people who care about you will not risk the possibility of offending you to share this information without it having at least some merit. Occasionally, there are those who are critical or don't share your faith in God's Word who will give you wrong advice, but a real friend or family member who has your best interest at heart should be heard and their concerns taken seriously. Uphold authority to your children and don't model for them that it is acceptable to consistently question those who are in authority. I'm not saying go overboard to please or appease others' concerns about your child, but recognize that we all have weaknesses, and sometimes we have an inability to see our child's behavior as it really is.

Recognizing that a child has willfully disobeyed, meet with them privately in a place away from others' ridicule or embarrassment, and tell them what they did and that they need to be spanked in order to remember that this is not the right choice to make. Spank them with a rod as the Word of God instructs (see Prov. 13:24). Discipline them hard enough that they are serious about never wanting to do it again, but not so hard as to be harsh. I consider a rod to be a switch, bendable reed, or smaller wood stick or dowel. It will sting but not do any lasting damage when applied to the padded area of the backside. It must bring pain to produce repentance, but never be done with harshness.

"*Foolishness is bound up in the heart of a child; the rod of correction will drive it far from him*" (Prov. 22:15 NKJV). Otherwise, the disobedient attitude remains and festers, producing more anger and resentment in the child. Repentance will bring an inner release and help remove the guilt of the action. One sound spanking administered in love for the child will render unnecessary hours of nagging, shouting, arguing, threatening, and do much less damage to their self-esteem.

Discipline gives the child freedom from being selfish and ruled by carnal behavior and attitudes of his or her emotions. Parents who are afraid to draw the lines on right and wrong and enforce them with discipline will allow their children to rule the home. The "foolishness of a child" is not able to rule a home, so consequently the child without boundaries does not feel cared for or secure and will eventually rebel against the parents who would not exercise enough authority to bring the child into a place of teachableness through discipline.

Children want and desperately need boundaries to feel secure and loved. The amazing thing is that parents who won't say no to their children's demands or discipline their misbehavior and wrong attitudes will end up having children who despise and reject them and their authority by the time they are around twelve years old or sooner. The very thing the parents feared came upon them, because they wouldn't heed the instruction of the Lord, and now their own child rejects their instruction. *"No discipline seems pleasant at the time, but painful. Later on, however, it produces a harvest of righteousness and peace for those who have been trained by it"* (Heb. 12:11).

For discipline to produce the results we are expecting, we must do it with love, consistently, and not when we are just inconvenienced or mad enough with our child to do it, and we must do it with a rod as the Word instructs. Finally, after administering the discipline needed, we need to utilize the time immediately afterward to restore our child by encouraging them that they are loved, forgiven, and accepted, then use it as a "teaching moment" while their heart is tender and softened by the discipline. We must not bring the incident up again in conversation or remembrance. Just as Jesus cleanses us from all unrighteousness and doesn't bring it up again, our sins being as far as the east is from the west, so should our attitude be about their misconduct. We don't discuss it with friends and relatives or remind them of it so as to shame them. They learn that we can be trusted with their deepest darkest moments, and that we are not trying to harm them or shame them, but we are actually working for their good to help them overcome sin and wrong attitudes and help them to become all that they can be.

If you have doubts about how to handle a situation, always ask the Holy Spirit for guidance. God's love is unconditional, but there are consequences for our choices, and so should our love be toward our children. We should teach them that our love for them doesn't change when they sin or do wrong, but there are consequences for their decisions. In doing so, they learn to receive love and correction as an act of our love. Our children actually learned to welcome correction.

One time one of our daughters came to my husband and said, "Daddy, I think I need a spanking because I did something wrong. I didn't tell you the truth." She actually welcomed the confession, repentance, and restoration that discipline brings. Ultimately, our goal is that when our children are grown and we aren't guiding them daily, their heart will have been trained to make the right decisions. As our children began to understand correction, Gary had a rule that if they came and confessed any wrong actions, he only required them to make restitution rather than being disciplined with a spanking. In this way, they were not fearful of punishment and came to us instead of running from the truth. We felt this helped them understand that they should go to Father God instead of hiding from Him when they did something wrong. Of course, we never allowed this to be manipulated.

As our children moved into their teen years, we had trained their hearts to be accountable, and the love-discipline relationship we had established gave them an inner desire to do what was right and to please us. The teen years were actually the most joyous in their upbringing. We had developed a mutual respect and enjoyed watching them blossom into adulthood. The time invested in the earlier years and consistent communication helped them seek our counsel instead of peers during the most pivotal time in a young person's life. They knew we had their best interest and future in mind, and they had learned to trust our guidance and input. I can't stress enough how important it is to start this from a young age. As many horror stories as I have heard about teens, I can honestly say this was not our experience. Rebellion doesn't happen overnight, and if a parent is connected with their children, any warning signs should invoke a parent's loving intervention and interaction. Parents must be a child's first place of counsel and care. If peers replace this role, trouble will soon develop.

If you have teens who are rebelling against you as a parent, let me offer some encouragement to you concerning how to rebuild and discipline them and prayerfully make up for some lost time. First, you will need to invest more time than discipline to regain the relationship. You can't "buy" their trust or bribe them with things. They need you. It is important that you are willing to make this the most crucial priority. Don't overreact to the situation, but remain calm and create a secure environment. If they are testing the boundaries of your love for them, the last thing you want to convey is that you are losing your head and they are now controlling you with their misbehavior.

The father should step into the role of disciplinarian, especially with teens. Again, time invested into them must be the stronger focus than discipline. However, a father should see to it that respect for the mom and the household rules is upheld. Not with yelling or demands, but with firm, calm correction and removal of privileges that go with the responsibility.

We maintained that with freedom comes responsibility. If the simple well-defined rules are not met, the privilege is not granted. A sample rule may be: If you want a cell phone, you must put it on the charger in our bedroom at ten o' clock and not misuse it during other times. We should also be careful not to give our young adults privileges they are not ready to handle. This sets them up for failure and oftentimes to be controlled by the privilege (i.e.: cell phones, iPods, Facebook, Internet, movies, video games, events, and certain friends). We never used church or church-related activities as discipline! There must be something else you can remove from their life instead of cutting them off from their spiritual influences and Christian friends. As much as possible, with any privilege you remove, replace it with time with you doing something they consider enjoyable. Reestablish your love and care for them and confidence that you are removing the privilege because they have not been able to handle it at this time. Talk about the answer and not the problem.

Young people must know that you still believe in them regardless of their mistake, because they often don't believe in themselves. Explain they will have other opportunities at a later date to reestablish their ability to make right choices. As with younger children, do not embarrass them or continue to rehearse their mistakes. Lectures will cause your child to tune you out but loving talks open hearts. Don't be afraid to take authority and maintain a strong role in your teen's decisions, friends, and influences and discipline through loss of privilege.

From training five children, I can assure you God's ways work and bring about untold rewards! There can be no greater joy than to see our children grow up and walk in truth! This is the product of parents obeying God's truths.

One of my rewards was that in the past year, our beautiful 25-year-old daughter, Amy, met a wonderful young man. Knowing the sacredness of a marriage commitment, she had kept her commitment to purity and to not date until she met the man whom she felt was the right one for her. The young man proposed to her in a very romantic way, surprising her as she stepped to the platform to lead worship at church. In front of friends and family, she shared the joy of the moment.

As a date was chosen for the wedding, with great excitement and anticipation Amy and I began to make plans. In a surprising and emotional moment, Amy asked me to be her maid of honor. At first, I laughed and thought she was jesting, but the look on her face told me otherwise. She said, "You have always been my best friend, so why shouldn't you be my maid of honor?" I can't think of a higher honor. On their wedding day she presented me with a beautiful ring and necklace that read, "My best stories begin with, 'One day my mother and I...'" As I witnessed the beauty and holiness of their wedding ceremony, standing as her maid of honor, I thanked God for His ways that bring peace and joy.

> Love is a mighty power, a great and complete good. Love alone lightens every burden, and makes the rough places smooth. . . . Nothing is sweeter than love, nothing stronger, nothing higher, nothing wider, nothing more pleasant, nothing fuller or better in heaven or earth; for love is born of God, and can rest only in God, above all created things.
> THOMAS Á KEMPIS

Loving Communication

Above all else, our love has to be the cord that binds it all together. Training and discipline without love is harsh and ineffective. Love can be demonstrated in so many ways. As parents, my husband and I have made plenty of mistakes, but our heart has always been to communicate our love to our children. As we have sought to follow God and let His Spirit deal with us in this and every area, we have been corrected by our Father in Heaven, and we've always believed He was correcting and leading our lives toward a good end. "'For I know the plans I have for you,' *declares the Lord, 'plans to prosper you and not to harm you, plans to give you hope and a future'"* (Jer. 29:11). Our children need to know that our heart is to do them good as well. Our love cannot be in word alone, but in deed as well.

The woman who has "IT" realizes she must live as an example to her children, while mentoring, loving, and disciplining them through her unselfish acts of giving.

One of the primary ways we show love is through communication. What are our actions communicating to our children? Are they our priority? Do we care what others think about us more than what our family thinks about our attitudes, actions, and behaviors? Day by day we are communicating something to our family about their value, their potential, their place in our hearts and lives. Words, physical touch, gifts, and acts of serving are the ways we share with others that they have value in our lives. Our children all need these expressions of love, but some of them are stronger needs in their lives. We should offer all of these methods of expression as Shakespeare wrote, "How do I love thee? Let me count the ways."

You can show a child love by speaking words of life and encouraging them consistently. As important as discipline is to a child, greater yet is the need for words of encouragement and positive belief. You can write these words in cards, notes, or messages on your home message board and email or speak them in person, over the phone, in a song, and on the voicemail, but by all means, share words of life! *"Death and life are in the power of the tongue, and those who love it will eat its fruit"* (Proverbs 18:21 NKJV). If you recognize and love the fact that your tongue has the power to speak life into situations and people's destiny, then you will love the results!

People aspire to the words that have been spoken to them or over them. The words spoken to us as children form the basis of what we believe about ourselves. As small children, we believe what those in authority tell us about ourselves. If we are told that we are stupid, talk too much, or that we're awkward, unattractive, and will never accomplish anything, we believe this. The opposite is also true. Understanding God's love for me and my children, I continually prayed for our children and asked God's wisdom for how to handle situations and challenges that we all face as parents. I have specific prayers I have prayed over each of our children that dealt with God's plan for them. One of my favorite Scriptures is, *"The Lord will perfect that which concerns me"* (Ps. 138:8 NKJV). I have prayed that God would perfect that which concerns my children. I often speak this as a release of my faith in God and His Word. It brings me comfort and reassurance that God is taking care of all the details. He has been faithful to do so.

I detest teasing that belittles another person. To get a laugh or approval at the expense of another person is a perverted form of communication. Some have been raised with this form of candy-coated criticism as a means to get attention from the person who is being teased or others joining in on the tease. Don't do this to your children, and don't let them do it to others. These words still convey a negative message even though they are delivered as a joke or putdown. There are many loving ways to share a laugh with your children. It's best to laugh at your own mistakes and not those of another.

We encouraged our children that when we are together, we are not rude to one another by plugging into an iPod or game unless it is for a short break on an extended trip. It deeply concerns me when I see young children playing hand-held electronic games at the dinner table in a restaurant or parents not involving their family in conversation. How can we teach them social skills and build relationships if they've learned to tune out family discussions?

Everyone needs a physical touch. Some more than others, but we all need to receive hugs, kisses, pats on the back, and to have our hands held in comfort. There is a message that says "I love you" without words when a person touches us in a way that makes us feel cared for. Babies who do not receive touch can actually die from lack of being nurtured in this way. Scratch their backs, tickle them gently, play with their hair while you watch a movie, hug them whenever you can, give them a kiss before they go to bed, and insist they kiss you as well. Affirm your love with touch.

And when they're teens, don't stop! Many times youth need touch all the more because of the insecurities they are facing as they grow into adults. Many times I believe youth start looking to someone of the opposite sex to meet their physical need for touch if they are not receiving the touch they need at home. We see so many 12 and 13-year-olds hanging all over each other, twined together as though they're one, looking for fulfillment and love in a dangerous place that often leads to premarital sex.

If your teen thinks it's not appropriate to show affection to you, now that they are getting "older," a teasing jest can break the ice. "Hey, where's my kiss? You're not too old to give your old mommy a kiss, are you?" It never fails to bring a smile from my sons, a little blush (and a hug or kiss). The highest compliment I ever got was from my almost grown sons who walked up to me and initiated a kiss on the cheek before they would go somewhere (and occasionally even in front of their friends!). And as grown men, they still show me affection. Wow! I know they love me. And all those years of touching, hugging, and back scratching pay off as they reciprocate to me what I have sown (or shown) into them!

This past Christmas, our 24-year-old son gave me a stack of red leather boxes. On the top, a note read: "Who is my mama?" Inside the boxes I found dozens of interesting items he used to relate a quality he observed in me each with a note he had created in his beautiful handwriting. They read:

> *My mama is a therapist; she is always willing*
> *to listen and impart.*
> *My mama is fun; she is the life of the party.*
> *My mama is a thinker; she has a sharp mind and*
> *can work out any problem.*
> *My mama was my driver; she has always made it a*
> *priority to drive me where I needed to be,*
> *burning rubber to get me there on time.*
> *My mama is in style; she always stands out and looks*
> *good. I'm always happy to claim her.*
> *My mama is a dreamer; she always believes and looks for*
> *the possibility of what could be.*
> *My mama is a nurturer; she has given me life and has*
> *shaped it.*
> *My mama is sweet and strong. She is gentle and loving,*
> *but will get in your face...in love. She won't take no*
> *for an answer.*
> *My mama is a learner. She always wants to gain*
> *understanding. She is also my teacher and guide.*
> *My mama is a writer. She is many things,*
> *including a writer.*

I'm not all that, but in my son's mind, I am! But the one that made me cry was when I pulled a zebra fabric umbrella out of the box with a note that read:

> Encouragement is oxygen to the soul.
> GEORGE ADAMS

My mama is shelter from the rain. She has been my protector, and nothing can stop her from her child in need.

There is no sacrifice or paycheck that could touch me like that.

Celebrate!

We have a tendency to take our children and the opportunities to enjoy them for granted that we often miss it. Whenever I hear a mom say she can't wait until the kids get back in school or move out, it concerns me. Cherish the time with your children, because it goes too quickly. And celebrate their lives, especially their birthdays.

David said that he would not give God an offering that cost him nothing (see 1 Chron. 21:24), and the principle is true regarding our children. A gift can be an act of serving with our time that we give as a gift, or it can be a physical purchase that we make to give that will hopefully make our children's eyes light up with delight. Either way, it is the effort and time that we take to make them know that we care. Our children need to be the greatest benefactors of our serving and gifts of love. I have always tried to make their birthdays and certain holidays super special. It is my way of saying, "You are special, and no one can take your place. I am not too busy to recognize that your birth is still special to me, and I will never forget the day you came into my life." The woman who has "IT" makes life a celebration for and with her family.

Even when we had very little money, I asked God to show me how to make birthdays special events. I was blessed to have a mother who did the same for me, and a father who paid for it! I saved ribbons, bows, and store displays from other events, planned theme parties for months, and then shopped at dollar stores and garage sales to carry them out. Some of the best parties I've thrown were when we had little money at all. A couple of times I had tea parties for my daughters and used real china, my old antique dolls, and had all the girls wear "dress-up clothes" and ring a bell on the table for the butlers (my sons) to serve them more food or drinks. They laughed and laughed and had a blast, calling the boys over and over to get something else. This was even fun for my boys, who wore their Sunday suits and ties and acted the part with enthusiasm. They all learned that when families work together to celebrate, it makes the journey more fun and the joys greater.

With five children and birthdays every year, I don't think there is a theme party we haven't had or a secret getaway we haven't tried to create. We have kidnapped family members and blindfolded them for fun to drive them to a secret surprise destination. We have had several surprise parties, and God has always given me the resources and special touches to make it memorable. I encourage you to turn life's struggles and work into celebrations of accomplishment and milestones of fun along the path.

Grow Their Faith and Guard Their Hearts

A positive tool we have used in our family to keep us in communication and on the same page spiritually is family prayer. I am not talking about a legalistic ritual, but rather an enjoyable time of going from one person to the next around the room and letting each child share challenges they are facing, requests of desires and needs they want to petition to receive from God. The children would volunteer to pray over different requests. Each person has their way of praying; some stand, some sit, some walk, but everyone is engaged in this time. Some of the most powerful prayers, encouragements, worship times, and the funniest times have originated from our children.

A very memorable prayer time for a different reason ended in outbursts of laughter. As I prayed over my assigned requests, unbeknownst to me, my son's ferret, which I have always been intimidated by, was loose. Running across the back of the sofa, it leaped onto the top of my head and held on. I screamed, and everyone except me lost it laughing as the skinny elongated rat held on to my head for dear life, and I thrashed around yelling, "Get it off!"

We also have a notebook where we record all of our family prayer requests, and at least monthly we review the requests, checking off the ones we have seen complete. To all of our astonishment, we have seen major answers to not only our prayers, but our children have also seen the goodness of God and the effectiveness of prayer. We always take time to praise God for all that He has done as we review these answers, and it builds all of our faith.

The destiny of each child's life is precious. We need to desperately guard their hearts from the pain and dysfunction of this world. Don't let television, movies, music, video games, and outside influences negatively impact your godly seed. You are the protection God has placed in their lives. Regulate how much and what kind of influences you open up your tender child's heart to receive. In our family, video games were only allowed on Saturdays when the boys were ages 10 to 17, and we didn't allow them to play video games before that age unless we visited an arcade as a treat. We didn't watch any movies that were stronger than a G or PG rating and almost no television. Most of these activities we did as family, so we were aware of what they were viewing. Occasionally, one of my sons would complain that others were doing "this or that," but now that he's an adult he thanks us for regulating these influences in his life. He also told me he plans to wait even later in life to allow his sons to play video games (smile). Instead of using entertainment to babysit our children, we were busy living life with them!

> Success is never final.
> Failure is never fatal.
> It's courage that counts.
> JOHN WOODEN

In our culture today, we give our children too much to fill their heads but not enough of the right things to fill their hearts. For that matter, we all could use a little less information and more heart revelation and relationship with our families.

God Always Has a Plan

If your children are older and you feel you have made mistakes that are not fixable, trust that God's grace is greater than your errors. We always see areas we could have handled better, but somehow God's *"love covers over a multitude of sins"* (1 Pet. 4:8). Pray and ask God's guidance to be able to begin again. If your children are at home, you can share with them the new direction God is giving you and set new standards and boundaries for your family. Share the vision of God's plan for family, focusing on the positive rewards of living life under His plan. Don't try to change everything at once without their understanding of your reasons and goals. Accept responsibility for any past misunderstandings, and help your children see your heart toward them is love and the changes you are making are to benefit them.

Whatever you do, don't dwell on the past. You cannot go back and live it again, but do what you can today. Pray and share the love of God with them. Don't preach at them, but bring healing to the relationship with love and kindness, and you might even share this book with them if they find themselves facing life without direction. Don't try to make up for the mistakes of yesterday by taking false responsibility for their decisions. You can't buy them out of trouble or continue to make financial decisions to help them out of consistently bad decisions. Life has a way of disciplining and helping us come to the end of our ways. If we shield our children from consequences every time they get into trouble, they will never come to this place. It would be better for them to endure some hardship for a season that would bring them to a realization they need God than to rescue them whenever they continue to repeat bad decisions.

I have seen many mothers who struggle financially because they are still "paying for" the poor choices their grown children make. I have prayed with many women who are destitute financially, and I usually find out they are using their money to take care of problems for irresponsible sons or daughters and oftentimes raising grandchildren as well. Honor God and His Word above your child. If you are operating from a position of strength spiritually, emotionally, and financially, you are in a much better position to offer God's help to them. Love them, but don't be manipulated into taking their responsibility. You will actually cripple them if you do. You do not need to bear the guilt of the past and try to pay for it today. Give God an opportunity to become their answer to trouble.

God has a plan for our children's lives, and He is able to reach their hearts in ways that we cannot. Trust His leading. Pray and dedicate your child to Him. There is hope in God.

get Money:
AND GIVE
IT AWAY!

7
get Money:
AND GIVE IT AWAY!

Let us see that we keep God before our eyes, that we walk in His ways and seek to please and glorify Him in everything we do. Depend upon it: God's work done in God's way will never lack God's supplies.

Hudson Taylor

As a young woman, I dreamed of making money and becoming very rich so my parents would be proud of me. The message I had adopted was that women should skip out on marriage and children and go after success, which was equated with having money at any cost. Fortunately, along my journey, God intervened and redirected my life and values. I've been without money, but once I found "IT," I've never been without a meaningful life purpose. Money doesn't define my purpose, but rather my purpose gives definition to what I do with money. Along the road of life with its lean financial times, I have found that I could still enjoy the happiness of following God's purpose, and later when money followed our vision, I was just as content. Money is merely a necessary tool, not a purpose. It must follow our purpose, and it can help fuel our vision, but money alone has never made anyone happy long term.

After Gary and I were married, we lived in Tulsa with no family and being fresh out of college had few friends in the area. We both wanted to be generous and support the work of God's Kingdom, so one of our goals was to become like the apostle Paul, whose business ownership as a tentmaker allowed him to travel and gave him the freedom to share the Gospel freely (see Acts 18:3). Our prayer was to believe and trust God to help us build a business as we helped Him in His business of advancing the Good News.

We started out in an older apartment, and our first Christmas tree was a gangly cedar we cut at the roadside, yet we were as happy as could be with the knowledge that God had a great future for us. We wanted to make a lot of money and be able to give a lot away too. I can't say our motives were 100 percent pure, but they were certainly innocent and a little naive.

It wasn't long before we realized that making money wasn't as easy as we thought. Gary worked in commission sales, offering insurance comparisons and replacing outdated and overpriced policies. This made him the target for criticism from others in the industry, and because he was so shy, he struggled to make phone calls and to find the courage to meet with people one-on-one in their homes, night after night. At first, being a new bride, I didn't want him to leave me; but once I realized there was no money if he didn't, I quickly began to encourage him to "get to work. Why are you home tonight? Don't you have any clients to see?" In one particularly slow month, I got on the phone and made cold calls while he was out. I set several appointments for him, and through those appointments we were able to hire new employees and bring in much needed income.

We had a sofa and coffee table that had been handed down from my parents, a cardboard box that I turned upside down and put a tablecloth on, some knickknacks, a few appliances, and we slept on a palette on the floor during our first months of marriage. Eventually, we saved enough to buy an unmatched mattress set at a discounter. But I was thrilled to start this adventure of building a business together, and I was sure we'd be rich by the time I was 30. When Gary came home in the evening, I had a candlelight dinner on our cardboard box table, and we would dream about the future.

I worked at a nice restaurant as the hostess and eventually as a waitress, so the tips kept us with enough money to pay utilities and buy a 99¢ burrito for dinner from Taco Bueno. Gary worked evenings, seeing our first clients. We sold my Mazda RX7 for cash, so I rode to work on a blue moped that was given to us as a Christmas gift. I still smile as I picture myself putt-putting down the road in my work uniform: black skirt, white crisp shirt, black apron, and bowtie.

> Make all you can, save all you can, and give all you can.
> JOHN WESLEY

Somehow we struggled through months of famine and occasional feasting. Of course, during the feasting months, we had to catch up on our bills from the months of lack. It was through such times we learned the lessons of life that would later make our dreams come true. Our characters got major overhauls as we learned to develop self-discipline and trust in God and His promises.

The Power of Dreams

I remember the first really specific desire (other than just financial survival) I put my faith into action to accomplish. There was a trip offered through one of our insurance vendors, a trip to a lush resort in Boca Raton, Florida. We received a video that highlighted the beautiful trip. By this time, I was pregnant with our first child, and finances were tight, with no chance of a vacation. I wanted this trip so badly that I watched the video every day for months. I made Gary watch it, too! He'd say, "Not again, Drenda."

To win the trip, we tried to break down our sales production into weekly goals, and I monitored our success. To our astonishment, when we not only set our goals but also broke them down into a week-by-week work management schedule, we began to break our past records. Halfway through the contest, we both realized we were falling a little short of the trip requirements, so I got my license and began to sell, too. At several months' pregnant and on the very last night of the contest, we needed two more sales to make the trip. I had an appointment on one end of town, and Gary had one on the other. We had to meet at the FedEx office with both sales closed or we lost the trip.

After much persuasion, I finally got my client to take the sale, but I only had fifteen minutes to make it to the FedEx office before they closed. If I didn't get there, all was lost. I didn't know my way around the area of town I was in, and with no GPS or cell phone back in those days, I prayed, "God, help me! I don't know how to get there from here, but I know You didn't get us this far to fail!" Adrenaline rushing through me, I was praying as hard and fast as I could to God. Suddenly, I spotted a FedEx truck in my rearview mirror. It came barreling past me, and I knew the truck was headed in for the night. I hit the gas and followed it in an exhilarating chase. We pulled into the parking lot with one minute to spare.

Gary was already there, peering out the window. I raced toward the storefront door as if I was running for the winning Super Bowl touchdown. I was fully prepared to push my now protruding pregnant tummy through the door if they tried to lock it. Once inside, I found out that Gary had gotten his sale, too! We frantically filled out our paperwork as I tried to humor the clerk who was ready to close down for the night. We finished. It was done. Now we just had to wait and make sure our calculations were accurate. Had we truly won the trip?

With only enough money to split a Coke, we celebrated our victory at a fast food restaurant. A few months later, we were in Boca Raton, mouths hanging open, savoring our first experience at a posh resort. I walked the lush manicured grounds and found every camera angle and sampled every adventure I had envisioned for almost a year as I watched the video. It was a sweet victory, and we were like two kids who realized that our dreams really could come true. Many

> Resolve not to be poor: whatever you have, spend less.
> SAMUEL JOHNSON

years of struggles to get by followed, sometimes severe, but we both always looked back to that event and knew that if we didn't give up and worked together, we found that *"all things are possible to him who believes"* (Mark 9:23). We could win!

Through the years, I have come to understand the power of dreams. Proverbs says, *"Commit to the Lord whatever you do, and your plans will succeed"* (Prov. 16:3). I learned that God really does delight in the prosperity of His servants. I have studied this in the Word of God and have seen over and over that God has a good plan for all of our lives, if we will engage Him in our lives. He cannot and will not intrude or force Himself on us, but He wants to be as much a part of our money and finances as He wants to be in our worship service.

A Generous Heart

Money is an integral part of all of our lives. We have to have it to live! That's why Jesus said, *"No one can serve two masters. Either he will hate the one and love the other, or he will be devoted to the one and despise the other"* (Matt. 6:24). We look to the one we think is our source for answers, which can be tricky, since we need money to live. Jesus said it best though, *"Man does not live on bread alone, but on every word that comes from the mouth of God"* (Matt. 4:4). Provision comes from following the teachings of the Word of God and is an outcome of godly choices, not the source itself. I have discovered that the need for money can be as great a temptation in a person's life as any. It is the "love" of money that is the root of all kinds of evil, not money itself (see 1 Tim. 6:10).

There are temptations with money on both sides, "having" and "not having" it. I have been in both situations, and I have found that if a person has a good heart, having money only magnifies that, giving them more opportunities to do good. But if a person's heart is greedy for money in itself, it will create more greed and opportunities to use it to do wrong. Money cannot define my purpose or be my master, but rather God's purpose gives definition to what I do with money. Therefore, to a good-willed person, having money is a great blessing, since *"it is more blessed to give than to receive"* (Acts 20:35). I must have something to give! And I must begin to develop a generous heart with what I possess today, or I will never be able to handle more. This principle applies to everything. I must use the tools and resources I have today in order to develop them into something greater. God never asks for what I do not have, but He wants to teach me how to use what I have and turn it into more.

When you have God's heart toward people, you will always have more demand for money than you have resources, because God's heart toward people is big. He wants to bless and give to His children. Nothing has taught me this more than parenthood. I want to see good things for our children. I am willing to do without things to make sure they have their needs met and enjoy themselves. When I see lack in people's lives, I want to fix it—orphans fed, homeless cared for, families able to take vacations together, single moms (and dads) able to provide for their children. The needs and wants are endless. I don't want just enough for me. I want plenty to give to others.

Love is expressed in the desire to give. *"For God so loved the world, that He gave..."* (John 3:16). At the same time, I do not want to give my children anything that they cannot handle properly and that would harm them in any way. As a parent, I always want them to advance and excel, but never at the expense of their character or choosing what is "right." Therefore I gauge what I can give them by the effect it will have on their faithfulness to remain true to the purpose of God using money and things to serve Him. If I know they can be blessed and bless others, there is no limit to all I want for them.

The woman who has "IT" realizes this Kingdom secret: As we give, we actually train our hearts to have a right attitude toward money and life. And as we become faithful with little, we can truly be trusted with more (see Luke 19:17). We started our married life with $6,000 of college debt, and even though our income was very meager, we found that God was faithful to His Word as we sought His direction and gave our tithes and offerings, as well as kept our hearts open to let God use us to help others as He directed. We concluded that our money was not ours—period. Rather, because God was our Source, "our Master," we could hold on to possessions loosely, and anytime He

> Money is a terrible master but an excellent servant.
>
> P.T. BARNUM

wanted to use our money, He could do so freely. Even though we often failed this test of our hearts, we learned more and more to be obedient, and as we did, our finances reflected His provision and overall success in life. The only times we had any other experience is when we violated His Word and did what we wanted to do without seeking His direction first.

Never Violate God's Principles

I have always been personally drawn to John 15 and, in particular, to verse 7 and 8: "*If you remain [abide] in me and my words remain in you, ask whatever you wish, and it will be given you. This is to my Father's glory, that you bear much fruit, showing yourselves to be my disciples*" [bracketed copy mine]. Early in our marriage we began to learn how to apply this teaching.

One such incidence was another trip Gary and I won through a business endeavor—this time to Acapulco, Mexico. However, this trip did not include free airfare, and we didn't have the money for tickets or even our house payment at that moment. We were in the process of learning about faith, so I prayed for the money for the airline tickets. Just before the deadline, a random offer came in the mail from a finance company that stated all we had to do was call and activate the offer and buy our tickets. I thought, *This must be God!* I would like to say we said no to the whopping 28 percent credit option, but with the lure of the trip and a lack of understanding concerning God's Kingdom, we activated the check and packed our bags.

So many times we ask God for things we aren't ready to receive, and without considering the consequences of our decisions, we take a shortcut, using a questionable method that violates God's principles. "*Satan himself masquerades as an angel of light*" (2 Cor. 11:14). Just because we have prayed for something and an answer seems to appear doesn't mean it is the Father's plan. We must learn to "abide in Christ," to listen as we pray, and come to know His voice and His ways. Then we will no longer be tossed to and fro by every circumstance of life and every credit offer.

Once we got to Acapulco, Gary checked the ATM every morning just to make sure we weren't bouncing checks. He was so nervous we couldn't relax, and I was physically ill during part of the trip. To add to our tension, there was political unrest at the time, and armed guards walked the beaches with machine guns. When it was time to go home, we discovered there was a tariff to leave Mexico. We had to borrow the money from someone to get out of there! When our flight landed in Texas, Gary said, "I could get out and kiss the ground!"

> A man's treatment of money is the most decisive test of his character—how he makes it and how he spends it.
> JAMES MOFFATT

It took us several *years* to pay off the loan for those airline tickets. The problem was not the destination, but the manner in which we got there! God wants to bring "whatever we wish," but unless we "abide in Him," those wishes can turn into a trap that mimics our prayers. We learned God's ways and eventually became debt free. Many years later, we received another trip to Acapulco debt free, stayed at the same resort, and enjoyed a very memorable time with great friends. This time it was by abiding with God.

Get Serious About God's Word

We continually passed and failed money tests, and with each one we learned more about God's ways and to wean ourselves from trusting debt. One such test came when we had recently moved to Ohio to do what we believed God had definitively spoken to us in prayer, "our end-time work." We believed that because we were obeying God in the move, everything would be quick and easy, but it wasn't. It seemed that with the move we were set back even further and barely making it financially.

One time I remember my mother calling and asking how we were doing. I said, "We're doing great, Mom." She said, "Is that so? Go to the refrigerator and open the door. What do you see?" (Thank God for moms who know when things aren't right!) With quivering lips I managed to sputter out the words, "A jar of empty mayonnaise!" as I choked back sobs and held them in my chest only to give way to their gasps.

To make matters worse, the night before we had attempted to use some free "kids meals" certificates at a local restaurant. It had been a long time since we had eaten at a real restaurant, so we thought if we could scrape enough change together, Gary and I could split a meal and the kids could eat free. We searched our couch cushions, old coat pockets, and under car seats until we scraped together twelve dollars in mostly change. We took it to the grocery store, converted it into paper currency, and went to the restaurant. I remember the hostess looking us up and down with what I perceived as a "we don't serve the likes of you people," then she said, "Unfortunately, there is an hour and a half wait." Our two children were too hungry to wait, so we walked out just as a rock concert let out at the convention center and people poured out into the streets. In the unfamiliar busy streets, Gary missed a red light, and the next thing we knew he was sitting in a police car, and the kids and I are crying in our old van. Little Tim said, "Daddy's not going to jail is he, Mommy?" We got a ticket that cost us almost $100. Through tears, we made our way to McDonald's on our remaining cash.

This was too much. I had never felt so hopeless, so ashamed, so dejected. Where was God? We were trying. But it wasn't God who had signed the papers that got us in debt for that past trip to Acapulco. It wasn't God who had signed the bank notes or bought the car tires on a credit card. We realized we had always thought debt was the way to meet our needs. It wasn't that we were frivolous, but we didn't ask God to show us how to meet the needs without debt.

This was one of the lowest times of our lives, and the only time I can remember thinking, *Maybe we have believed a lie. Maybe God really doesn't care about us.* I fought self-pity, but it was getting the best of me. It was the only time our groceries were completely gone, and we had no money. But God did help us that day. Gary's mother knew something was wrong and showed up at our apartment and took me to buy groceries. I didn't think about God using a person to "help us." I resolved then that we would become people who "helped others." The pain of not having food was the worst. No one should be without a way to take care of their children. We were never really hungry, but this was bad enough for me to know that nothing good comes out of poverty, except for "coming out."

I determined that day, as I remembered Scarlett O'Hara say in *Gone with the Wind*, "As God is my witness, I'll never be hungry again." There had to be an answer. We must be missing something. I determined to find out what. I found out that when we get desperate enough to get serious with the Word of God, the answers were there all along.

The Dead Sea is a dead sea because it continually receives and never gives.
AUTHOR UNKNOWN

Psalm 1:1–3 reads, *"Blessed is the man [or woman] who does not walk in the counsel of the wicked or stand in the way of sinners or sit in the seat of mockers. But his [or her] delight is in the law of the Lord, and on His law he [or she] meditates day and night. He [or She] is like a tree planted by streams of water, which yields its fruit in season and whose leaf does not wither. Whatever he [or she] does prospers"* (bracketed copy mine). I wanted to live this Scripture.

When You Sow Much but Reap Little

Our third child, Thomas, was born, and with more opportunities to sit in the months that followed, I studied the Bible and listened to the Word of God on tape. One night I decided to stay up until I had an answer from God. I prayed for direction, for His deliverance, for answers that we desperately needed. "I am not going to bed, God, until You speak to me!" I had learned to trust God enough to get into this journey of marriage and children, but the area of finances with a family was new. Before I committed my life to God's plan, I just worked hard and expected money would come. Now, raising a family, I had to decide between going to work and letting someone else daycare my children or me answering the call to be an at-home mother.

Just after midnight that night, God took me to Haggai 1:5-6 (NKJV), *"Consider your ways! You have sown much, and bring in little; you eat, but do not have enough; you drink, but you are not filled with drink; you clothe yourselves, but no one is warm; and he who earns wages, earns wages to put into a bag with holes."* This stood out because it seemed as though the harder Gary and I tried to earn a living, the more obstacles we faced, and it was always a struggle.

Then I read on, *"'You looked for much, but indeed it came to little; and when you brought it home, I blew it away. Why?' says the Lord of hosts. 'Because of My house that is in ruins, while every one of you runs to his own house'"* (v. 9). Historically, I realized God was speaking to Israel as a people, but I could also see the parallel and believed that God was speaking to me through this Scripture as well. The people of God were experiencing severe lack, and it was because of their disregard for God's Kingdom and a stronger desire for their own. In our struggle, I was so focused on the problems we were dealing with that I really didn't think as much about the big picture. God had situations going on in His Kingdom with His children all around me, but until I had been in this situation, I really didn't see it. It was more about me, more about what I needed. When there is lack or need, we tend to focus on ourselves.

Haggai 2:7–9 (NKJV) states, *"'I will shake all nations, and they shall come to the Desire of All Nations, and I will fill this temple with glory,' says the Lord of hosts. 'The silver is Mine, and the gold is Mine,' says the Lord of hosts. 'The glory of this latter temple shall be greater than the former,' says the Lord of hosts. 'And in this place I will give peace.'"* And it adds, *"Is the seed still in the barn? ...But from this day I will bless you'"* (v. 19).

Suddenly, I realized that our lives were no longer to be focused on us, but that God's heart was big toward His children, and there were problems in God's family that I wanted to help solve. I wanted to sow the seed of my life into helping people with their finances and their marriages. I knew in that moment that God was going to take our trouble and show us how to help others out of debt, teach them how to make it through marital challenges, and how to raise a family in tough economic times.

I woke Gary up and said, "God just spoke to my heart. We are going to help people with their marriages and show them how to get out of debt." He looked at me through a sleepy fog and said, "I wish He would show me how first." Then he rolled over and went back to sleep. I was puzzled as to why he was not as excited as I was. I had received an answer that ignited hope in me. I could handle these daily pressures as long as I knew there were answers, and it wouldn't be this way forever. I prayed for Gary to be encouraged as he slept with my hand on his chest, and it wasn't long before he came to me and said he was changing direction in business. He was going to teach people how to get out of debt. Every day was still an up-and-down battle, but I had hope in my heart that God had a plan for us.

With renewed hope, I prayed for some items the children needed and found them all at a garage sale. As I drove through the country, I prayed about living there. That evening I talked to Gary about our finances and told him I would live wherever we needed to live to get out of debt. I asked, "If we can't afford $600 a month rent, what can we afford? $300?" He said, "Yes, that's what we can afford."

The following morning as we drove to a church, I spotted a country farmhouse way off the road. At the roadside a "FOR RENT" sign with a phone number sat in the field. I called the number when we arrived home, and to our astonishment the 1800s farmhouse was for rent for $300! With one bathroom, three bedrooms, a shotgun living room, small parlor, and kitchen with back porch, it was an extreme "fixer-upper." It had cracked windowpanes with vines growing through and a cellar with creepy crawly bugs that would frighten the toughest of men. Regardless, it was our price tag!

We took it and began to clean, paint, strip wallpaper, and stain hardwood floors by night and work by day at our business. We made the children a floor palette, and they would sleep while we worked. After two weeks and much exhaustion, we were able to move in. It was a high-pressured time, but it looked as though God had heard our

> Where your pleasure is, there is your treasure. Where your treasure is, there is your heart. Where your heart is, there is your happiness.
>
> AUGUSTINE

prayer for deliverance and we were on our way. Gary said, "If you can manage with this house for three years, we should be in a position to do better by then."

Living in the farmhouse had many joys, but also many trials. I think of it as my wilderness experience, where many character issues were worked on in my heart, and I was tested again and again with defining moments. I had to recommit over and over to the decision to get out of debt. I often felt like a hypocrite, because we had now developed our business to help families get out of debt, but we were still in debt! As we learned more and more to share with our clients, we benefited from our new knowledge and revelation. The more we learned about the bondage that borrowing causes in our lives, the more we grew in our conviction not to use debt.

The Power of Delayed Gratification

The initial feeling of bliss we get when we make a new purchase, whether it's a car or house, clothing, a boat, or whatever, has a short-term euphoria, but if we make those purchases with debt, it's not long before we are buried in pressure. Proverbs 10:22 (NKJV) states, "*The blessing of the Lord makes one rich, and He adds no sorrow with it.*" There are so many schemes and devices of the enemy to put us into servitude to debt or anything else we have made a master of in our lives. Today's idolatry is selling our soul to debt payments and then being so strapped that we don't have the freedom or time to have relationships with God and the people we love.

Gary came to me one day and said, "Drenda, I need to repent to you. I am sorry. God has shown me that I have trusted in debt more than His Word. I haven't taken the time to learn how He does things in His Kingdom. Instead, I have learned how to juggle credit cards, debt payments, and rely on debt whenever we have a need."

We both made a commitment that night to go cold turkey and refuse to obligate ourselves to any more debt payments. "If we go down, we go down. They will write on our tombstone: *Gary and Drenda Keesee went down trusting God.*" We didn't go down, but our new commitment was tested.

One evening as Gary left from an appointment, the client followed him out of the house, where our old blue van with 200,000 miles sat parked. As Gary waited for the client to leave, he finally had to start the van, which puffed a smoky blue haze. The client was a part-time mechanic and insisted Gary let him check it out.

He informed Gary that there was water in the oil and that the head gasket needed to be replaced. Discouraged, Gary talked to God as he drove home. "I don't have the money to fix it. In this condition, I wouldn't feel right about selling it to anyone else. And I owe more on it than it's worth. I just wish the thing would burn up."

Before he reached his office, paint began to bubble on the hood of the van. He thought, *What is that?* The spot got larger and larger. He pulled into the parking lot and watched in amazement as the hood burst into flames. Overwhelmed by what he was seeing, he thought, *God, You heard me! This thing's on fire!* Then he realized, *I better get out before I burn with it!*

He ran to the fire station that was two blocks away and reported the van "on fire." Fifteen minutes later a fire truck, sirens and all, barreled into the parking lot with several firemen. Apologetically, a fireman told Gary how sorry he was it took so long to get there. Outwardly, Gary was still in shock, yet he was half-excited on the inside that God had actually heard him. He called me with a "you're not going to believe what happened" story. Amazingly, after our insurance paid off the money we owed on the van, there was enough to also cover one of our credit cards that we were being threatened by collections!

We were thrilled God had come through in such a dramatic way. I teased Gary, "Moses had a burning bush, but we had a burning van." Then we realized that we didn't have a vehicle for our family. We prayed for a new van and had a very generous offer from a kind relative to give us the down payment for a new van. Gary lined up the paperwork, but all night neither of us could sleep. We thought about the commitment to not sign for any more debts. In the morning, I reluctantly asked Gary how he felt about buying the van, and he told me he was hesitant. He didn't want our family to do without, and I had not wanted to insult his desire to provide for us, but we both concurred that this was not the answer for us. He called the dealership and told them we would not be purchasing it. We both felt relieved, but now what would we do for a vehicle? We prayed again.

In addition to caring for our family and helping Gary with his business, I dabbled in buying and selling antiques on the side. I really didn't know much about antiques, but I had placed calls to retirement homes and offered to buy antiques from persons moving into retirement. I happened to get a call that day from one of the home representatives. He had an entire storage area full of antiques and wanted me to give him a quote to purchase them. I made a few contacts and lined up $500 to buy the antiques. My commission on the sale items at auction made enough to purchase a used station wagon. I drove it for a year, and at that point we had enough cash saved to buy a van just like we had prayed for a year earlier.

The woman who has "IT" has learned the key financial lesson to delay gratification of purchases as long as possible. With cash in hand, we have freedom to bargain for the best prices. Whenever I am tempted to be impulsive with a purchase, my husband reminds me, "They still make them!" In other words, we are tempted with deals when we fail to realize that there will always be "things we want" and "deals to be had." We should never let the desire of the moment jeopardize our future. Debt provides us with instant gratification, but we often don't count the cost of the impact it will have on our future. Through faith and patience we inherit the promises of God (see Heb. 6:12). Our dreams and desires need to be held in check with the correct timing. We can marginalize our options as we leverage our lives with debt. "Things" are meant to enhance our lives, but not to control our destiny. Freedom is always better than "stuff."

During this discovery time, I would pray about things we needed or often wanted, and to my astonishment, if I would be patient, it always came, some faster than others. Instead of grabbing a credit card, I learned to pray about all things, and it was fun to watch it come through God's way. We attended an auction where there were five beautiful prototype china cabinets for sale. They were very nice, and at $800 they were well below their original cost of $2,500+. I begged Gary to bid on one. He looked at me and said with his usual level headedness, "Drenda, does that meet our financial goals? Remember: They still make them." I knew he was right, but I wanted the cabinet. I let go and prayed instead. The cabinets sold, and we left, but this time I didn't feel sorry for myself. I was able to put my desire in God's hands.

> Think of what you do when you run in debt; You give to another power over your liberty.
> BENJAMIN FRANKLIN

Later that evening, we received a call from the auction house, since we knew the owner. They had another china cabinet that they chose not to run because it was missing the crown molding across the top. But after the auction they had found the crown in the lower drawer and wanted to know if it was something we would want to buy at $400. I looked at Gary with submissive yet eager anticipation. He said, "That is in our budget, and we can do it." I could see that by letting go and trusting God, He was teaching me it wasn't that I couldn't have beautiful things, but rather I just needed to keep it in perspective. It is still one of my favorite pieces of furniture, not just because of its beauty but also because of its story.

The Law of Sowing and Reaping

As we committed to get and stay out of debt that way, many friends and people didn't understand our commitment. Some said we were taking it too far, especially when we had lived in the farmhouse for almost nine years rather than our original projection of three years! But as we got completely out of debt and saved cash, we were able to do some amazing things with our lives. I am convinced that much of what we have been able to accomplish would not have happened without the commitment and follow through to stay free from financial bondage.

Women who have "IT" know that God always gives us provision as we make our way to our promise. We should never despise the day of small beginnings, since every endeavor starts small (see Zech. 4:10). Our business started small, but as we grew both spiritually and in knowledge of financial and faith principles, our business grew. We began to get vision, and because we were not strapped financially, we were able to act on ideas to further our vision and company. It grew and so did our income.

Practical "common sense" mixed with spiritual principles has made the difference in our finances. The truths in God's Word are designed to set us free and keep us free. Coupled with understanding basic financial concepts about how money works and staying out of debt, we were able to build a storehouse of wealth that enabled us to be generous. That's the foundation of true security. God's economy is always in great shape, regardless of what is going on in this earth-cursed financial system.

One of the principles we enacted was the law of sowing and reaping. We had committed to making our lives count, living not just for ourselves but for others as well. Beyond the desire to be generous, we recognized there was more to giving. I posted Scripture promises in various places around our home to remind us that God not only delighted in our giving cheerfully, but He also rewarded it.

The Lord has been mindful of us; He will bless us... (Psalm 115:12 NKJV).

And God is able to make all grace (every favor and earthly blessing) come to you in abundance, so that you may always and under all circumstances and whatever the need be self-sufficient [possessing enough to require no aid or support and furnished in abundance for every good work and charitable donation] (2 Corinthians 9:8 AMP).

A generous man will prosper; he who refreshes others will himself be refreshed (Proverbs 11:25).

Let them shout for joy and be glad, who favor my righteous cause; and let them say continually, "Let the Lord be magnified, who has pleasure in the prosperity of His servant" (Psalm 35:27 NKJV).

Whoever sows sparingly will also reap sparingly, and whoever sows generously will also reap generously (2 Corinthians 9:6).

We can give of our time, talent, and our treasure, but we must involve our money to truly give our all. There are three types of giving we have discovered. Being generous to those in need is clearly the heart of God, and He rewards those who take care of the poor. Ministry in its purest form is to take care of widows and orphans and "minister" to the hurting (see James 1:27).

Proverbs 28:27 promises that "*he who gives to the poor will lack nothing.*" God will repay this type of giving, and it is so important for us to give to those in need to keep our own hearts tender and humble.

Coupled with this type of giving, we have also discovered the principle of sowing our finances into ministries that are impacting our lives. When we have needs and desires, we look for those who have a ministry that speaks to our hearts and a special gift or anointing from God to impart to us. We minister to others through our generosity, but when we give into the ministries that touch our lives, we are able to receive from them. This is a scriptural principle we can see throughout the Word of God. The wise men gave to Jesus, the greater, and received from His ministry (see Matt. 2:11). The widow at Zarephath gave Elijah the prophet a cake she made from the last of her food, and as a result, instead of dying, she ended up living and flourishing (see 1 Kings 17). As we have purposely sown seed to reap a harvest that we need, we have seen amazing breakthroughs and provision come to us directly from God's promises.

We began to apply this principle and watched our "barely getting by" income rise to the place where we were truly able to be generous on every occasion. The more we reaped, the more we sowed again and again. We became very specific about the harvest we were "planting" to receive. In Philippians 4, those who had sown into Paul's ministry were commended for their giving and given the promise as recorded in verse 19, "*And my God will meet all your needs according to His glorious riches in Christ Jesus.*" This ministry of giving and receiving is also covered extensively in Second Corinthians 9. It is a grace that comes from God's ability, but we enact it through our giving in faith (with belief in the promise). Our giving actually sets a law in motion that allows God to bless us. The apostle Paul said, *"Not that I am looking for a gift, but I am looking for what may be credited to your account"* (Phil. 4:17).

The beautiful thing about God is His ability to take an area that is a weakness in our lives and transform it into strength. From the weakness that almost destroyed us, God raised us up by His Word and made our financial struggles into a springboard of ministry, a place where we could share the hope and promises that changed our lives.

We enjoy giving to those in need and sowing into those whose ministry is anointed to speak into our lives in areas we have needs, but we also give on a weekly basis of our tithe to the local church. Malachi 3:10 says, *"'Bring the whole tithe into the storehouse, that there may be food in my house. Test me in this,' says the Lord Almighty, 'and see if I will not throw open the floodgates of heaven and pour out so much blessing that you will not have room enough for it.'"* The tithe sets God's protection about our lives that the enemy will be rebuked or kept from our lives, and then we

> No one is really consecrated until his or her money is dedicated.
> ROY L. SMITH

can sow beyond our tithe to increase our harvest. Tithing was something that we can trace back to Abraham who gave a tenth to the high priest Melchizedek (see Gen. 14:20) long before Moses brought it as a law to the Israelite people.

Apparently, God taught this principle of giving to Adam and Eve after The Fall in order to be able to counteract the earth curse. God's promise that He will pour out a blessing that we shall not be able to contain and His ability to rebuke the enemy for our sakes is contingent upon the tithe. Through the tithe, we give God the legal right to affect our finances and overcome the earth-cursed system of poverty, which has yielded thorns and thistles since The Fall. Jesus wore a crown of thorns, and He bore all of the earth curse at the cross, but we enact His power in our finances through our obedience to give. It is finished and paid for, but we must release our hold on money so that as we give, it shall be given unto us.

Open the Windows of Heaven

As we gave ourselves to seek first the Kingdom of God and His righteousness, all the things we needed were supplied (see Matt. 6:33). By giving of our finances, we opened the windows of Heaven so God could bless us, and sowing into ministries determined the measure or amount of our harvest. We combined these spiritual truths with self-control and sound financial principles that we found as we sought God's direction. We came out of debt, and one day our time to leave the farmhouse came, and we moved into a new home that we had prayed for and sowed to have for our family.

Our finances had increased to the place where we paid off all of our debt and had saved almost $100,000. As our desire to help people by sharing all that we had learned grew, Gary and I started to pastor a group of wonderful people with whom we had shared answers to their needs. We did not need to receive income from the church, because our company supplied our needs, as the apostle Paul's tent-making business had supplied his.

Additionally, we felt strongly to take a step of faith to offer a marriage conference in our area as an outreach. Gary and I decided to personally underwrite the conference as a seed to build our home.

We rented a beautiful hotel ballroom and together with this band of believers hosted the conference. At the close of the conference, we ministered in a session about forgiveness and restoration. Across the room, couples wept and rocked each other in a picture I will never forget. It was so rewarding to see the transforming power of God heal couples' marriages. It truly was more blessed to give than receive. With the joy of the conference in memory and the excitement of giving, I almost forgot that we also believed God to do something for us as we were doing for others. He didn't forget, however.

> The problem with our giving is that we give the widow's mite, but not with the widow's spirit.
> AUTHOR UNKNOWN

Within two weeks of the conference, we were contacted by a couple in the church who had no knowledge of the seed we had given for our home. They were looking for land and said, "We have a property that you need to see. It felt like it was for you when we saw it." Several months later, we were able to purchase the property. We had asked God for at least 50 acres, since Gary especially loves to walk and hunt the woods, but it had to be close enough to town that I would not feel secluded from stores and civilization. This property was exactly the right mix of everything we needed, and we were able from our business income to completely pay for it within two months.

With our fifth child almost a year old, we were feeling the pressure to move from the farmhouse, and yet at the same time we had perfect peace as we labored in ministry and trusted God. Our goal was to pay for the new house over a long period of time and use cash only, but one night I felt an urgency that we needed to start the house in the fall instead of wait until the following spring. Gary agreed with my strong "nesting instinct," and we began work on our home in October.

After the basement was excavated, we stood in it, shaking and crying. It was one of the most exciting and humbling experiences. It was hard to believe this was our house! The house foundation alone was larger than the entire farmhouse. After almost nine years and much change in our personal ambitions, faith, and character, we were being promoted by God. We were overwhelmed with thanksgiving as we began to see that God's faithfulness to give as we gave to Him was far greater than we had even imagined. *"Now to Him who is able to do immeasurably more than all we ask or imagine, according to His power that is at work within us"* (Eph. 3:20).

I operated as the general contractor, and throughout the winter building months we continually saw faith provide answers to the decisions, finances, and help we needed to keep our business developing, the church growing, and our home built. In the spring, we got a call from the farmhouse landlord who said that after all these years he had sold the farm and needed us to be out in two months. We labored relentlessly to get the house to the place we could occupy it by the deadline. On July 4, we moved into our home with freedom, knowing that God had directed our steps. We finished the house as we lived in it, paying cash when possible to minimize our loan. Many times we could have paid the partial loan off, but in our eagerness to give to our new love, the ministry, we delayed over and over. In the end of the seventh year, our dream home was completely paid for. In our spirit, it was done long before that. We never struggled to make a payment.

Making Your Finances Work

As Gary and I have assisted people for 20-plus years with their finances, one of the major things we have observed in families is that the majority of women are handling the finances while they try to be moms, wives, and often a source of income. I am not saying that a married woman should not be involved with the finances, but the emotional makeup of a woman was not designed to bear the stress and pressure of this area alone. When a married woman takes this responsibility, she assumes the pressure associated with it, since we women are "fix it" people. Women were not designed to do it all. Even though we are great at multitasking, our hard drive goes into overload and something has to give—usually our peace and well-being.

When Gary and I married, I was used to keeping my own finances and wanted to handle the finances. I liked the feeling of being in control and having the freedom to do what I wanted. Gary didn't welcome the pressure of the finances and was happy to give it to me. At first there was minimal responsibility with it, but as we started acquiring debt and having children, there wasn't enough income to meet the outgo. Gary calls it "the five-year path to slavery." Young couples start out with big dreams and ambitions, but in five years or less they find themselves buried in debt. In my case, between answering collection calls, juggling bills, trying to help in our business office, and being a mom, it became an extreme emotional roller coaster ride for me. I personally feel the pressure of finances accounts for much of the discouragement, antidepressant use, anger, frustration, and emotional outbursts that plague so many women.

When we bought our first house, rather than get the "happy ever after" I thought came with it, I felt the crunch of a great financial weight. With two children under the age of three, I tried to do it all, to be super woman, but the pressure overwhelmed me. Then one day I lost it. I had an emotional explosion comparable to a volcanic eruption. It wasn't pretty. I yelled at Gary, ran out of the house, slamming the door, and sat in our yard crying and feeling deeply ashamed of my anger and rage.

I dealt with it as a sin issue, and God cleansed and freed me from it, but Gary and I sensed God had a practical solution for it. God called Gary to be the provider and protector of our family, and it was time for me to turn the finances over to him. I had to release the controls and trust this area to God and Gary. We started doing our finances more as a team, and he took the lead role and main responsibility. He sought my counsel, and together we found an arrangement that utilized our roles best. As he did, the pressure to provide fell squarely on his shoulders, and he could handle it. Meanwhile, a peace and joy came to me as never before, and I began to truly enjoy my role as a wife, mother, homemaker, and business helper to my husband.

An older woman gave me some good advice. She said, "Early in my marriage, I thought I knew more than my husband, and I tried to lead. But let me warn you, as you get into the next season of life, you will want to be able to lean on your husband's strong shoulders. If you don't encourage him to lead in the earlier years, he will never develop the experience to become a leader." I am so glad I took her advice. If I didn't give Gary the opportunity to lead and second-guessed or belittled his ability, he would never have the confidence he needed from me to become that man.

As married women, we should be part of the financial decisions, but not control or carry them. Gary and I never make any large financial decision without the agreement of each other. He keeps the finances in order and handles the day-to-day pressures, and we work together on the big picture and common goals.

For newlyweds and couples without children or women working part-time with children, I recommend you do not make purchases using any debt device based upon your income. Use your income for extra goals such as saving or special purchases outside of your financial obligations. Gary and I have talked with many tearful moms who want to stay home with their children, but she can't because they leveraged themselves with debt before children entered the picture. You may think you want to continue working outside the home full-time after the baby, but make sure you leave yourself an open option, for I often see women decide they want to leave the workplace or work from home in their own business.

Some of the biggest financial messes we have seen have been in the finances of single women. One of the main reasons I have observed for this is compulsive and impulsive spending and using purchases as an emotional comfort...much like a chocolate fix. My best advice for single women is to not go into debt. Utilize cash for a used car rather than a new car on payments. Live below your means and save for a day when you may want to make other career decisions or to withdraw from the work force altogether. Whatever your age, you will want the freedom to make choices to raise children, visit grandchildren, and do social and ministry work as you desire. If you find yourself in serious debt, get a plan of action to get out of debt and stay out of debt as you exercise God's Kingdom principles. If you struggle with compulsive spending, make yourself accountable to someone you trust who has excellent financial well-being because of their disciplined habits. Don't make a contractual purchase without discussing it with them first.

Whether married or single, exercise extreme caution concerning weighty financial decisions. Weigh the price of the item with the get Money: And Give It Away!

value it will have in several years and the payments you will still be making on it. If at all possible, do not use credit or debt for any item that is depreciating. The payment will remain long after the item has lost its value. Establish a cash reserve of at least three months' income before you make any contractual purchase. Don't dip into it for a fun purchase or spending spree. It is an emergency cash fund, not a cruise fund. Remember, even if something is on sale, if you buy it with credit, you will pay eight to ten times more than the sale price, so its not a sale unless you can pay cash for it.

> No one would remember the Good Samaritan if he'd only had good intentions. He had money as well.
>
> MARGARET THATCHER

Realize with the purchase of a home, there is so much more financial commitment than just the purchase price. You will want to decorate and furnish it, complete repairs, buy appliances, and the list goes on and on. Count the cost before you build or buy the house. If it is going to strap you, don't do it. Owning a home is a great blessing and building a home can be a very rewarding experience, but only in the right season and with financial soundness.

I pushed God and my husband to buy our first home, and we were not ready for it. I forced it by borrowing not only from the bank but also from my parents. Within two years the economy collapsed, and we owed more on the house than it was worth! It was a learning lesson for me that God eventually delivered us from. The next time we rented for nine years until we were able to pay cash to build a home and pay it off in less than seven years. We always had more equity than debt in it. With a volatile market and America's debt-laden economy, the best policy is to owe no man anything except the debt of love (see Rom. 13:8).

176 • she gets It !

I can't cover all the financial issues that come up regarding women, such as for divorced women who must deal with the financial woes inherited from the poor financial decisions of the marriage or for widows who are being pressured into investing their money. For more information I trust, I recommend my husband's book, *Fixing the Money Thing*.

Partnership With God

The more we learned that God wanted to advance us and how to use our faith to believe His Word and receive the promises, we kept raising our business income goals so we could give more and do more for people. He gives seed to the sower and bread for eating (see 2 Cor. 9:10). We have seen Him increase our store of seed, and as we are faithful to give, He keeps moving us into greater faith battles where we are able to conquer new territory and grow in our giving.

In time, not only were we able to pay cash for the things of life and give freely, our family started to sow into missions and had the joy of traveling across the globe to minister in Albania, Philippines, Europe, Canada, Mexico, Native American reservations, and all across the U.S. These were dreams we had in the early years, but now we were living them! We know now that our needs, wants, and desires are important to God, and He has blessed all the work of our hands as He promised to do. We must work, but it is a joyous labor of gathering with Him.

The woman who has "IT" finds that the greatest joy of all is being in a partnership with God in every aspect of business, family, and finance. He is a wonderful Partner, and we both reap the benefits of working in the "family business." Not only did we enjoy personal successes, we went on to begin an international television program to share this message of the Kingdom, reaching 550 million households. Our church also grew and was able to build a seven million dollar project. Discovering God's Kingdom and faith in His Word changed our lives.

God wants to bless your finances. As you join Him in the family business of touching lives, He will more than amply reward you with inner joy and the financial blessings of your inheritance. All good fathers want to share an inheritance with their children who have labored along with them in the family business, and so does your heavenly Father.

get Friends:

INVEST YOUR LOVE IN OTHERS

To Love and Forgive

Real Friends

Covenant-Based Friendships

Honesty in Friendships

Dealing With Misunderstandings

In the Good and Bad Times

The Best Friend Forever

8
get Friends:

INVEST
YOUR LOVE
IN OTHERS

A friend loves at all times...

Proverbs 17:17

rowing up without a sister but with two brothers, I always felt I could relate to guys better than girls. I had many girlfriends, but I was never comfortable sharing my deepest feelings and problems with them. I was quick to help when a friend needed me, but hesitant if I needed to confide in someone myself. My mother was where I went for advice.

Perhaps it began with the older mean-spirited girl who lived next door and made fun of everyone, including me (at least that's the perception I had as a 12-year-old), but I came to see most females as competitive, jealous, emotional, and "not to be trusted." My impression was that from birth we girls were destined to be pitted against one another for the attention of teachers and then the males around us. To complicate matters, my high school girlfriends were the top students, and we all competed to see "who" would be valedictorian. I received that honor, but not without paying a price.

Several months before I was to give the graduation speech, a few of my "friends" went to the principal and tried to have me removed as the valedictorian because I had graduated early. He called me into his office and told me about their effort to strip me of this honor. I was crushed. Then he said, "I have gone around to fellow class members and asked them their opinion. The only people who have a problem with you holding this honor are your close friends, so I have decided you will give the speech."

I was grateful for his decision, but it didn't displace the pain I felt over their betrayal. They were actually competitors, dressed up as friends. I had worked hard for all my school years, and this was my payoff? It somehow didn't seem important anymore. Fortunately, this was one of the incidents that caused me to turn to God only a few months later. I came to the conclusion that working for honors or success was a hollow accomplishment if it required hurting someone else.

Unfortunately, most of us have experienced the ugly side of supposed friendships. A friend of mine who teaches school told me that the worst fight she has ever witnessed occurred between two girls who had been friends. And, you guessed it, it was over a guy! But in our driven world, women are competing for positions at work as well, and some are quick to drive a dagger in another's back if it means a promotion, money, status, or a sale. It's no wonder we aren't sure who to trust or how to find meaningful friendships. Without trust, there is no room for vulnerability or real relationship.

I always longed for a sister and to have a truly close friend, but I was too afraid and insecure to trust very much of myself to others' scrutiny. I had lots of friends, but kept them at some distance. After I put my faith in Christ, I went to college, where I met two sisters who lived in the dorm room next to me. They shared makeup, clothes, jewelry, and lots of laughter. I thought, *Wow! What would it be like to have a real friend like that?* As sisters, they had the freedom to be themselves. There was no risk that the other would find a fault and expose it to others, then leave the friendship. Theirs was a friendship for life, but there was more to them than that.

Even though they were incredibly close to each other, they were kind to others as well, not cliquish or competitive, as were so many other girls I had seen. They both had amazing clothes, but were quick to be generous. One of them offered to loan me a dress for a formal dinner. They took a sincere interest in helping me look nice. Being away from my mother and with few relationships in a new place, it was comforting to have someone who cared. This friendship was different. I saw that Christ-centered friendships could be different from the ones I had experienced. There was a steadying force in both of them. They had "IT."

We've all had good and bad experiences in friendships. I have come to appreciate that everyone needs a BFF (best friend forever). I'm glad to say that we can all have that kind of friendship! The woman who has "IT" has the Best Friend anyone could have, and it is truly forever. Once we get that area secured, befriending others is so much easier.

> A true friend is someone who thinks that you are a good egg even though she knows that you are slightly cracked.
>
> BERNARD MELTZER

To Love and Forgive

No other area of life has taught me more about friendship than ministering in the office of a pastor alongside my husband. When Gary and I started getting a strong revelation of God's Word in the area of freedom in finances, the call of God was stirring in both of us. A wonderful group of people gathered around us, much like the destitute men who assembled around David in the cave of Adullam (see 1 Sam. 22:1). We poured our lives and teaching into many of them, day after day and week after week. We were struggling but had begun to taste of the promises of God. He had unveiled some wonderful truths to us about faith and coming out of debt, and we were beginning to see the impact.

As we shared these principles, they were working in all of our lives. A year later, it was clear that God wanted more from us than to merely share these financial truths as friends. Our home was an open door, and with many telephone ministry calls, house meetings, and eventually church services, we grew very close to many of them. God dealt with us about the office of the pastor, and we received the encouragement from those to whom we had ministered to say yes to His call to pastor.

As a few years went by, we saw great fruit in our lives and in their lives, marriages, and families. We loved them so much and wanted to see them win more than we wanted it for ourselves. As our businesses grew, we paid off our debt and saved enough money to pay cash for land for a house. Eventually, we were able to leave the old farmhouse and begin to self-contract our new home. We thought everyone would be happy and celebrate with us, since they had seen our plight in the farmhouse and knew our willingness to serve their families. We saw a new home as a ministry tool and encouragement to everyone of God's faithfulness. However, some of the friends I felt the closest to ignored me and acted bothered that we were finally able to own a house of our own. They didn't owe me anything, and I wasn't looking for their help, but I wanted to be able to share my joy with them.

Week after week we labored contracting our house, but some friends seemed indifferent. Some circulated words of gossip about us and second-guessed our decision to contract our home ourselves, which we did to keep our costs down. Others would come bearing tales of what "so and so" said about us. I didn't see them as any better friend or confidante for their tattling.

I was excited to have the home God promised me, but I was saddened there was no one to rejoice with me. *How could friends treat me with such disregard after all that we had poured into helping them? Didn't they know my heart, or had they already forgotten our commitment to them?* What was supposed to be a joyous time became a painful discovery for me.

Human nature, as Jesus said, tends to envy. We struggle when we see others get something if we think it may not happen for us. This really comes down to our fears and failure to trust God's love for us. God began to show me the times I had been jealous of others and had acted unbecomingly in situations. He reminded me of the times I had treated *Him* this way, working for His Kingdom halfheartedly and not sharing His joy of the Kingdom with enthusiasm. I recalled the times I complained or mumbled when I had to work through the night helping someone in need. He even said, "Did you do this for them or for Me?" I realized that ministry was about loving when others didn't choose to love in the same way that Jesus loved me.

As He revealed this, I had a choice. I could harbor resentment and get bitter, or I could choose to get better. I knew that God was not going to be able to continue to bless me if I got a wrong attitude. He had done so many wonderful things to share His reward with me, so wasn't that enough for me to let go? I was hurt, but the only one who was going to suffer for it was me.

When someone hurts us, we tend to rehearse the offense over and over, to repeat the words or actions that caused our pain. The more we do so, the deeper the wound and the more powerful its emotional hold becomes. The offense grows and so does the misunderstanding. Offenses are always trying to lure us away from truth and relationship. When we take an offense into our soul, we stop the blessing of the Lord, and we create a blockage in our heart where we cannot give or receive His goodness. "*He who covers over an offense promotes love, but whoever repeats the matter separates close friends*" (Prov. 17:9).

Instead of letting it drive a wedge between us, I decided to love and forgive my friends. I put myself in their place and began to realize how easy it would be for me to feel envious if the tables were turned. The woman who has "IT" understands the frailty of humanness and that when afraid or hurt, we tend to hurt others, so she responds with forgiveness.

One night as we worked late on the house project, a couple from the church that we didn't know very well came by. They just showed up. We didn't know how they even knew where to find us. Night after night, they showed up with iced tea and their assistance. I was grateful for their help, but what I really appreciated was their friendship—to be able to share our dreams with them and to know they shared our excitement. We have been friends ever since.

> Two persons cannot long be friends if they cannot forgive each other's little failings.
> JEAN DE LA BRUYERE

Real Friends

Having friends is a crucial part of our lives. Without them, it's easy to feel a sense of loneliness. We have no one to share our challenges and victories. When we are faced with decisions that are difficult, we all need someone to be a sounding board for us. We want someone to celebrate "us" when times are good. Real friends are the ones whom we can be ourselves with, and they truly "get you." Although they know our weaknesses, they celebrate who we are as a unique gift to the world. They believe in us and our purpose, and they share common beliefs about life and God. Ecclesiastes 4:10 says, *"If one falls down, his friend can help him up. But pity the man who falls and has no one to help him up!"*

These friends can be rare to find. We have to be careful in friendship and slow to move into relationships that have a commitment of our time and, even more important, "who" we are. Entering into any relationship has its blessings and perils. Even though I am friendly to everyone, I have learned I can only have friends in close proximity to my life who understand me and want to see me fulfill my destiny in God. And yet, even the best of friends are going to step on our heart occasionally. Misunderstandings happen in every relationship, but it's worth the risk if it's the right kind of friend.

Jesus was no exception in His humanity, and the fulfillment of His calling and destiny was dependent on friends—both those who truly loved Him and others who only served Him for what they could get out of the relationship. Regardless of whether they proved to be fair-weather friends or true God-sent relationships, Jesus reached His destiny, and many of the friends who failed Him were there for Him after His resurrection, while others left Him and went their way. He had those who were His "close personal friends," such as Peter, James, and John, and then those who were His disciples, being mentored by Him.

As Jesus' disciples grew in common vision, He said to them, "*I no longer call you servants, because a servant does not know his master's business. Instead, I have called you friends, for everything that I learned from my Father I have made known to you*" (John 15:15). Those who started out serving Him became those with whom He shared the Kingdom as true friends. They had often aided Him and occasionally attempted to thwart Him in His mission, but they became sincere and trustworthy. Yet when He faced His darkest moment in the Garden of Gethsemane (see Matt. 26:36–46), He still had to do it alone, but not completely. Father God proved to be His closest companion as He faced His mission of the cross and the darkness. There are times when we want friends to be there, but God, and God alone, is our answer and refuge. He is enough in those moments.

I have always found this a fascinating Scripture: "*But Jesus didn't entrust his life to them. He knew them inside and out, knew how untrustworthy they were*" (John 2:25 MSG). We know that Jesus had to "trust" His disciples to minister in His behalf, to do tasks needed for the ministry, and so on. As I have gained more understanding about human nature, I believe Jesus didn't trust His mission or assignment to any man's interpretation, opinion, or criticism. He had to personally account for the vision's accomplishment. He knew He couldn't rely on the fickleness or insecurities of people, their weaknesses and lack of understanding, to dictate His choices. He had to do what was right whether His friends went with Him or not. He may have to do it alone.

Always aware of this possibility, He trusted Father God completely and exclusively. It was His cross to bear.

There are times when we all are faced with similar choices, whether to please people or to obey God. It's not always easy to say yes to God at the expense of rejection, pain, or even the loss of a friend. The fear of man or woman is a trap. A real friend wants you to obey God and will not manipulate you to get what they want out of the relationship at the expense of you failing your assignment. "To thy own self be true." To be true to ourselves, we really must be true to God. He made us, and He knows the purpose and destiny for our lives. No other person can be trusted to carry out our mission to its fullest. People will come and go in our lives, but the purpose of God for each of us will endure, if we remain true. And real friends will endure as well.

It's important to keep the perspective that Jesus "*is a friend who sticks closer than a brother*" (Prov. 18:24). If we experience betrayal or rejection from friends, God's love and commitment to us is unwavering. He is never too busy to listen or to help us. He is always seeking our best and encourages us with hope. Even when we have blown it in the worst way, He believes in us, and even His words of correction are restorative. Forgiveness and commitment are His ways, and we have His friendship when no one else stands with us. All of us will have moments that test our hearts and motives to see if Jesus is our first love, our closest companion—will we trade Him for something or someone who is temporary? Jesus said, "*You are My friends if you do what I command*" (John 15:14).

Situations in friendship arise that cause us pain, and we have all caused friends pain as well. We have been betrayed, and we have betrayed. That's why forgiveness and commitment are important to be able to stay in any relationship and endure the storms of rocky times in friendship. God wants us to choose our friends carefully, and we shouldn't stay in any relationship where the other person is continually trying to harm us or keep us from our potential in Christ. A real friend sees our potential and encourages us. Love doesn't seek its own but rather the other person's good (see 1 Cor. 13:5).

> A real friend is one who walks in when the rest of the world walks out.
> WALTER WINCHELL

Covenant-Based Friendships

There must be a place of agreement for us to truly open our soul to another person. *"Can two walk together, unless they are agreed?"* (Amos 3:3 NKJV). We can be friendly and reach out to anyone in order to share God's love, but the people we open our hearts to must be of deeper fellowship. The Greek word *koinonia* means "fellowship." It makes me think of two fellows in the same boat who are rowing in the same direction, headed to a common destiny and vision. I have exhorted youth for many years that they will become the friends with whom they hang out. *"Bad company corrupts good character"* (1 Cor. 15:33). If we try to throw someone a rope to help pull them into our boat, we must be very careful not to lose our own bearings and end up drowning or shipwrecked in our faith.

If your friends are in a different "ship" (kingdom), it's much easier for them to pull you out of yours and cause you to go overboard. *"What fellowship can light have with darkness?"* (2 Cor. 6:14). I can't have real "fellowship" with someone who is against the very Kingdom of God that I represent and from which I draw my entire life force and purpose. I can love someone, pray for them, and reach out to them with God's love, but friendship that is covenant-based isn't possible. We simply have two different agendas. A woman who has "IT" doesn't compromise God's truth for any relationship.

We cannot afford to confide in and open our souls to a perspective that can destroy our foundation in Christ. We can minister to anyone, but be a confidante of very few. *"A righteous man is cautious in friendship, but the way of the wicked leads them astray"* (Prov. 12:26). I have not seen anyone go astray who didn't do so without the help of a "friend." That's why friendships are to be entered into very carefully. Jeremiah 9:5 states, *"Friend deceives friend, and no one speaks the truth. They have taught their tongues to lie; they weary themselves with sinning."*

In Ezra 9:12, God's covenant people were instructed, *"Therefore, do not give your daughters in marriage to their sons or take their daughters for your sons. Do not seek a treaty of friendship with them at any time, that you may be strong and eat the good things of the land and leave it to your children as an everlasting inheritance."* God warned them to avoid marriage or friendship with anyone who did not share their covenant with Him if they wanted good things in their lives and to protect their family. Notice that friendship was the same as making a treaty or covenant relationship. To make a covenant with someone is to state that all I

> A friend can tell you things you don't want to tell yourself.
> FRANCES WARD
> WELLER

have is yours and all you have is mine. We truly don't understand the depth of this type of friendship with all of our shallow "on again and off again" relationships. King David went so far as to honor his friendship with Jonathan by taking care of Jonathan's son Mephibosheth long after Jonathan's death (see 2 Sam. 9).

Covenant-based friendships were built around loyalty to God and each other and were intended to be lasting.

Honesty in Friendships

Friendship requires honesty as well. If we truly love someone and are committed to their well-being, there are times we must honestly disclose to our friend what we know is causing them harm. There is a right timing and way to do this, but it is never easy to share if we think it may damage the relationship. We must, however, care enough to confront the issues that harm them or others. I believe we would all grow into maturity if we could receive the truth about our lives from our friends. *"Wounds from a friend can be trusted, but an enemy multiplies kisses"* (Prov. 27:6).

A real friend is honest with us, but takes no delight in jabbing us with the truth. I know that my heart and motives are right when I don't want to hurt my friend and have spent more time praying about the issue than I have rehearsing their fault or error. Prayer, timing, commitment to the relationship, and examination of our own motives are crucial to such an intervention. There should be no pleasure in having to "wound" a friend with truth. But it is the truth that sets us free. If we have real fellowship with them, our commitment to them must be greater than the fear of sharing a problem we know is detrimental to their growth. *"Rebuke a wise man and he will love you"* (Prov. 9:8).

"Speaking the truth in love" (Eph. 4:15) requires a far greater commitment to friendship than the typical immaturity we see in "friends" who gossip about a problem in someone's life. Rather than go to the person, they gather an arsenal of others to expose

their friend's weakness. This isn't friendship; it is slander. I refuse to spend time with those who do this to others or me. We have all made these mistakes, but we must grow past immaturity and become true followers of Christ and real sisters in the Lord.

The woman who has "IT" doesn't get caught up in silly gossip or attempts to set others straight while she has perversity in her own heart. I have discovered that most people who stir up strife against others are actually acting out of their own insecurities and are judging others through the plank that is in their own eye (see Matt. 7:1–4). For example, if I have a problem area in my life, the tendency is that I judge others through my own motives and tend to see them through my filter, assuming they are acting out of the same motivations. If a plank blocks my sight, I can't see things as they are. I see with a distorted view.

We have seen many situations of this type of distortion as we have ministered over the last 21 years. We once had a young man and his family who came to our church and were always struggling to buy groceries and pay their bills. He kept telling my husband how wonderful he was and that he had no trouble coming under such a great leader. However, this man was trying to mask his own heart with his flattery. He had always had difficulty with leadership, whether it was an employer or a pastor; and as a result, he had moved from job to job and church to church.

This man desperately needed the teaching that my husband offered him, but he became offended at the truth. He then began to secretly draw a group together to "pray" for us. These were like-minded people who had orphan spirits, constantly desiring attention and recognition, and who drew others after themselves by finding fault with their leaders. While there's no question we weren't perfect leaders, our sincere desire was to do right for them and toward God.

Not all of the people drawn into this situation had bad intentions; they were just easily drawn into devilish snares. I have found that couples that seem to have marital issues, where the husband doesn't lead properly and/or the wife doesn't respect his leadership, often fall into these kinds of snares. The Bible talks about deceivers who worm their way into the homes of "weak-willed" women who are given to gossip and faultfinding (see 2 Tim. 3:6). The enemy especially wants to damage young believers by these types of schemes. If the shepherd is attacked, the sheep scatter (see Mark 14:27).

It wasn't long before this man was so convinced that his accusations against my husband were true that he called Gary with a list of twelve things he was supposedly doing wrong. Meanwhile, this young man didn't even hold a job. Most of his accusations dealt with money, which was the thing he needed most, yet he wouldn't work for it! He demanded to know how much Gary was paid by our church, and much to his shock, Gary answered, "Nothing. The church pays me nothing." The man stammered as he conceded that my husband should probably be paid "something."

Because this man was manipulative in his ways to get money, he judged my husband likewise. His accusations, all of which were ludicrous and based on his own perception and concocted notions, were dispelled one by one. He claimed we were "after the money," when in truth he was jealous over our success. My husband was not only doing the work of a minister, but he was paying for it from our businesses. This man accused us because his own attitudes toward Father God, leadership, and money were wrong. Gary was very gracious to him and quickly let him off the hook for his wrongdoing. However, it wasn't long before he was offended again and left. Even though we knew it was best for our church, we felt sad because he needed the understanding of God's goodness and character that he rejected, and he continued to drag his beautiful family through turmoil.

> Friends cherish each other's hopes. They are kind to each other's dreams.
>
> HENRY DAVID THOREAU

Dealing With Misunderstandings

In friendship, there are many times we just need to overlook situations, keeping in mind that "*love covers over a multitude of sin*" (1 Pet. 4:8). The woman who has "IT" realizes she cannot control the actions of others, but she can control her response.

There have been times when I knew a friend's actions were out of character. I chose to trust her heart and look past the actions rather than be quick to judge her current puzzling behavior. I didn't go and confront her, since this was not typical of her. Instead, I recognized that there must be something out of the ordinary that required my understanding and willingness to see past my feelings and come to her aid. I have often said to myself, "They didn't mean to do that. They're just under pressure or hurt about something."

Misunderstandings also occur between the best of friends. We must stay committed to believe the best in our friends unless we see their intention is repetitively for our harm. Then we must let go. We can't change the person's choices, and we can't live in the shadow of their assaults, but most of the time, "*a gentle answer turns away wrath*" (Prov. 15:1).

I once had a friend who had some prickly ways. I believe she really had a good heart underneath the sternness, but almost weekly we would have complaints about her offending people from church. My husband said, "Drenda, you must talk to her about this for her own good and for the church," but I was terrified to do so. We were young in the ministry, and she could be intimidating. After much prayer, I mustered the courage to address my concerns with her. She got rude immediately and told me, "That's just my personality. I can't change," and I left aggravated.

Some other problems occurred with her that seemed to be directed at me. I was so frustrated that I could see myself slipping into an offense with her. I prayed about what to do and felt very strongly that God told me to buy her a gift and express my love toward her as well as to accept responsibility for any offense our conversation may have caused. My response was, "What? Why should I buy her a gift? God, she was in the wrong!" Reluctantly, I obeyed and began combing through store aisles for a gift. As I did, something happened. I found my offense release. I began to think of all the times she had done nice things to help others. Now, I actually wanted to "give" to her.

When I delivered the gift, she wasn't home, so I left it between the screen and door, positioning it with the card just so-so. As I gave the gift, I no longer felt reluctant to bless her, and a genuine love for her welted up inside of me. It was as if God gave me a glimpse of His great love for her. I, too, felt love. I was free from offense, regardless of how she chose to respond. I felt happy instead of angry.

That week she came to me and in humility thanked me for my gift. She softened and said, "You did not owe me anything. It was actually me who should apologize to you." I was overwhelmed to think how easily I could have turned against her and misjudged her heart along with messing my heart up, too. Love and forgiveness keep us free in friendship and help us maintain our own hearts and attitudes. A woman who has "IT" is quick to forgive others and seeks reconciliation whenever possible.

> Friends are like angels who lift us to our feet when our wings have trouble remembering how to fly.
> AUTHOR UNKNOWN

In the Good and Bad Times

If you know me as my family knows me, you know that I have a crazy side that likes to have fun, and sometimes I get carried away. I don't mean to. I just find that letting my hair down is good for me. We don't need any outside stimulus, such as alcohol or anything else, to have a good time! I have laughed in restaurants with groups of friends to the point of tears, and I'm sure if the waiter didn't know better, we seemed drunk! I love to laugh and will chose a comedy over anything that makes me sad. We create an atmosphere to foster friendship when we can laugh together and, when appropriate, cry together.

Friendship is about sharing and giving. It's about investing into the lives of others so that all of our lives are enriched. Friends are born for adversity (see Prov. 17:17), to help get us through the rough times, but we are cemented together when we can share fun together as well. Friendships can't be about "heavy" or negative things all the time! We've all been around someone who dumps their problems on us or talks badly about others whenever we come into contact with them. We want to avoid them because we know what a "downer" their conversation will be. No one likes a one-sided conversation that revolves around hurts and how they've been rejected over and over. Or even worse, a conversation that leaves us feeling dirty because they have slung mud on others.

I have met women who say they have no friends and no one ever invites them to do things. The Bible states that someone *"who has friends must himself be friendly"* (Prov. 18:24 NJKV). Characteristics of a "friendly person" are a smile (no sour faces, please), willingness to communicate with others (it's hard to know a silent person or an excessive talker who only talks about herself), consideration of others' needs and opinions (self-focus is very unattractive), and investment into the relationship (giving and receiving, talking and listening). There should be giving and receiving in every friendship. If people seem to avoid you, you should be asking yourself why. If you're alone, then throw a party. Get your eyes off of yourself and start giving to others. You'll have more friends than you can handle!

One time I was driving in the car with a friend who always tends to be on the quiet side. She has a listening ear, and I have a tendency to talk, sometimes too much! However, on this day we sat in silence. Finally she said, "What's troubling you?" I said, "Why?" She said, "You are too quiet." She was right. I was troubled and under great pressure. I didn't want to burden her with my situation, but because she knew me, she perceived something was wrong. I was glad she did, because I knew she was trustworthy and my concerns would go no further than her. I also knew she was committed to pray and would sincerely seek my best. I could trust her.

There was another occasion in which I called this same friend to share a great victory. But once I called, I picked up on the sadness in her voice. She had had a very painful thing happen, and I immediately went into "friend to the rescue" mode. I spent the day helping her through the problem. Later in the week, she learned of my good news and asked, "Why didn't you tell me?" I said, "I forgot about it when I saw my good friend in need." We both smiled knowing that she would respond the same way for me and had done so many times. *"Rejoice with those who rejoice; mourn with those who mourn"* (Rom. 12:15).

Because of the demands of ministry, I have had to place at the feet of Jesus some of the time I would spend in friendships. I love my friends no less, but we have taken a leadership role as their pastors. This was tough for me and for my friends in the beginning. Before we were buddies, but with the change I knew it was more valuable to be their pastor than their best friend. I couldn't share sensitive details about people, and I knew that the office along with our family demanded much of our time and efforts.

They still encourage me and do helpful things to support the ministry work we are doing. I don't feel I can reciprocate the way I want, but I know their heart is to serve and not to manipulate my time or attention. I appreciate their sensitivity to the position I am in and their willingness to be involved, even though it has changed the dynamics of our relationship. I love them all the more because of their understanding. And I am blessed to see them "make disciples" as their lives have become busy about our Father's business as well. One day, our Father will throw a big party in Heaven for us all to enjoy, and I am sure we will do a lot of laughing!

> We cannot really love anybody with whom we never laugh.
> AGNES REPPLIER

The Best Friend Forever

Friendship is one of life's greatest blessings. Things come and go, but people are eternal. What is the value of a friend? Zechariah 13:6 says it best, speaking of Jesus, *"If someone asks him, 'What are these wounds on your body?' he will answer, 'The wounds I was given at the house of my friends.'"* Jesus was willing to give His life for us, His friends. It was His friends, including all He would one day call His friends, who wounded Him. It was our sin that necessitated His wounds. One of His closest friends denied Him and another misjudged and betrayed Him. He simply said, "*Friend, do what you came for*" (Matt. 26:50). As was true of Judas and Peter, Jesus knew we would not always be faithful to Him. It was our transgressions that ultimately nailed Him to a cross. Yet on that cross, He said, "*Father, forgive them, for they do not know what they are doing*" (Luke 23:34). His love and desire for our friendship cost Him everything. "*Greater love has no one than this, that he lay down his life for his friends*" (John 15:13).

The woman who has "IT" recognizes that she can have a best friend forever in Jesus. He has paid for her friendship with His life. He will never leave her or forsake her. He always knows her heart and believes in her. She is never truly alone as long as He is the lover of her soul. Flesh and blood will disappoint, but He will never let us down. That's a real BFF.

get Balance:
FITTING IT ALL TOGETHER

Living by the
Highest Priorities

How to Live
in Balance

Boundaries

Adopt New
Life Strategies

9
get Balance:
FITTING IT ALL TOGETHER

Things that matter most must never
be at the mercy of things that matter least.

Goethe

As the pendulum swings, many women are beginning to question the previous generation's priorities that put careers before family and money before purpose. Many women who have already lived the emptiness are looking for a way to help their daughters and themselves sort through the propaganda and return to meaningful relationships. But in a time when life continues to march on quickly and most have grown accustomed to life on two incomes and running constantly to juggle schedules, how do we return to a simpler time where we can relish the important and sift through the temporal? The answer is balance—prioritizing our purpose and letting everything else take care of itself.

Trying to juggle so many things in our lives can leave us tired and sometimes feeling as though it's hopeless to manage all the priorities of family, finances, church, school, career, and on and on. If we're not attentive to our true priorities, it's easy to lose sight of where we're going. To begin with, we must establish what is truly important in life. With frequency, we should reassess our priorities and decide if what we are choosing to do with our time aligns with our life purpose. Every time we face a decision, we should evaluate it in the light of our priorities, goals, and overall purpose.

My priorities are in this order: my relationship with God, my husband, our children, then our family's provision (vocational calling, business, full-time ministry), church ministry, and friends. Notice that my relationship with God and obedience to Him are separate from church in priority. Seeking God's Kingdom first brings all the other things added to my life in their right priority and direction. As I have God's guidance and stability in my life, I am better able to be the wife, mother, minister, and friend, which are also great priorities. The woman who has "IT" draws strength from God's love and gives it to those she loves.

> If we take care of the moments, the years will take care of themselves.
> MARIA EDGEWORTH

To analyze whether we are living and giving ourselves to our highest purpose, we must ask some tough questions. How do I spend my time? Is there an important area I am neglecting? In ten years, what do I want my life to look like? In twenty years? In forty years? When I stand before God, will I be prepared to give an account for my life? Am I on course? Who or what choices are helping me toward my life purpose? Who or what choices are influencing me away from my priorities? Is the house or second car worth the financial sacrifice or time away from my children? Is the travel aspect of my career a death sentence for my marriage? Are the children in a setting where God is their priority? Are we growing in love with our Maker every day? Is the extra income worth the sacrifice of moving the family away from their grandparents? Analyze and eliminate. Then add whatever is missing to help you reach that destiny. All of these are tough decisions, but the answers can make the difference in whether you arrive at your destination.

Living by the Highest Priorities

Our lives need the balance of caring for ourselves and those under our leadership. We are made up of three parts: spirit, soul (mind, will, and emotions), and body, and we cannot neglect to care for any of these areas without affecting our entire being. Since we were designed to live out of our spirit, we need to draw life-giving nourishment from God and His Word as a daily priority. This strengthens our mind (thought life), causes our will to align with God's will, stabilizes our emotions, and finally helps bring life and health to our body as the temple of God. I am also responsible to demonstrate and provide for my children, in the same balance, guidance, and provision. If I give them a great education or they become triathletes, but I fail to help them see their devotion to God as a first priority, they will experience imbalance in their lives.

Everything I do should be a ministry to the Lord, including being a wife or parent. I have seen many ministers prioritize the ministry over their wives or children and end up losing them for neglect. I know people today who will not step foot in a church because they felt they had to compete with the church or God for the love of their parent or spouse. I know men who have lost the love of their wives, not to adultery, but to the "other woman" of their ministry calling or business. How does a child compete with God, if God is the reason Dad is never home? Keep in mind that this is a false perception. God never asks us to destroy our families to follow Him. Parenting is ministry. Being a great spouse is ministry! When we see our lives from the aspect of the Scripture, "*For in him we live and move and have our being*"

(Acts 17:28), we will not be as easily drawn away from our calling to our families. We should never leave our children with the feeling that business, church, or any ministry continually has precedence over them.

Years before we became pastors, Gary and I ran into an acquaintance who started telling us all that he was doing "for God." He was leaving his wife and children at home to go across the country to attend a Bible school. My husband asked him how he would support his family for those years and what impact that would have on them? He was flippant in his response and stated he was leaving them behind for the Kingdom of God. Then he asked us, "What are you doing for the Kingdom?" It was a pointed question, intending to shame us into feeling insignificant, since we were "only taking care of our family, building a business, supporting our church, and paying our taxes." It wasn't long before he lost his wife to adultery as well as his relationship with his children. He blamed her and moved on. Ultimately, the "ministry" and God are so often blamed for these types of foolish choices that He never asks us to make. The Bible clearly teaches us that if we do not provide for our own families, we are worse than an unbeliever (see 1 Tim. 5:8). And if Jesus told the disciples to not forbid the children to come to Him, that such is the Kingdom of God (see Mark 10:14), He obviously values those who devote themselves to their proper care.

We can also put our vocation or friends above our spouse and children. I have seen both men and women leave their families to hang out with their friends to the ruin of their home lives and marriages. An occasional break with friends is great, but when it becomes the priority, trouble will come. Business has its demands, and there have been times when Gary and I have put business and ministry as a top priority to accomplish a task, push through a barrier that would benefit our family, or complete an assignment that was ministry-related. You can shift your schedule and devote more time to one area or another, but there has to be a deadline when you return to your other priorities.

> If we want to be fruitful, we need to make spending time with Jesus our number-one priority.
> JOYCE MEYER

I feel that many of the midlife crises that occur in men and women come back to priorities and the feeling that somehow the important things in their lives never were accomplished. So at middle age, with the children graduating from college and leaving, many people are troubled by what they never achieved or accomplished. If we tell ourselves, "One day I will take a meaningful vacation with my family" or "When I retire I will have time to…," we keep delaying the important at the expense of the current demands of life. There is a time to delay the gratification of purchases and anything that will strip us of our freedom to control our destiny, but spending time with your family is not one of those delays. At times, going through the day-to-day priorities can seem routine or mundane, but quality time really does come partly from quantity time. Being there for the ones you love helps to produce a bond that is strong.

How to Live in Balance

Women ask me from a practical standpoint, how do you balance so many priorities and keep them in balance? Let me be clear: You won't always perfectly balance it. There are days when one area or another will demand your time, and you have to give attention to it. We just need to keep the balls in the air as we juggle some of life's challenges, and as we see an area that is getting out of balance, we must stop and give it the priority it deserves. There are trade-offs and exchanges we make between our priorities to balance what is most crucial in the season we are now trying to navigate.

For instance, I was writing a book that was supposed to be finished before we left for a break at the beach with our youngest child. I wasn't finished and found myself writing on the trip. She came in while I was writing and asked me to walk down the beach with her. The book was important, but she is my priority. I set it aside and took the walk. If we aren't careful, we can be busy all the time.

For every person who disregards family priorities, there are those who use their children or family as a reason to never do anything outside of the family. I call that "the other side of the ditch." If you aren't diligent with business or don't attend or volunteer at a church, and you use your family as the scapegoat, your family will not get a clear picture of proper priorities. Families are stronger when there is a commitment to attend church regularly, give of themselves in service, and to have spiritual guidance from a caring pastor. Children must also see the value of a work ethic in their parents.

As you pray, ask God to show you how to manage your priorities and those of your family as well. I have had God speak to me about my children and specific needs they were experiencing. He would direct me to spend some extra time with them or show me that we needed to pull away as a family and take a break or vacation. Over the years, we have developed a pattern of flow that helps our family manage our life together and to stay refreshed. While your family pattern may not look like ours, get a pattern or family living system that will guarantee you are living your priorities.

This is the personal protection plan that has worked for me and my family. In the mornings, I pray and read my Bible before I get out of bed. Every night, I pray as I get ready for bed. I also practice God's presence throughout the day, talking to Him as needs arise or as I have moments alone. I check on the news or read *The Wall Street Journal* to keep up with the world around me. If I need a break or feel I have neglected myself lately, I take a hot bath and use it as a time to think and pray. I do something physical every day, whether it's a walk or playing with the kids. Sometimes I exercise, but not religiously. I eat a larger lunch and smaller dinner and try to stay away from eating sugar (except on vacation).

Gary and I have a date or at least one meal alone every week. We have at least one meal a day with our family. I am surprised how many families do not eat together at all. Mealtimes are special, and as I have traveled around the world, I have noticed that we Americans are much poorer than the Italians and French and most other countries when it comes to enjoying our meals together and having good conversations with one another. Ball games, school activities, working overtime, and almost everything else take precedence over our priority—family. We have to learn to say no to activities that will replace our family life if we can't manage to work them in without somehow stealing the precious time we have with our children.

We have one day a week that is "family day" for everyone in our family. On that day, we don't do things with others as a rule, and we don't allow anyone to schedule anything else on that day. We established this pattern with the children when they were young, so it was not a problem to manage it even when they became teens. They looked forward to being together. Every once in a while, Gary and I have failed to say no to an outside situation, and our children have called us on it. If we had to travel without the children, we have rescheduled a few family days; but for the most part, we keep family day sacred. Whether at the beginning or end of family day, we try to pray together.

Every 90 days, we take a break (three days at least) with our family. Our motto is: Work hard; play hard. While we are on break, the children always insist that Gary and I go out to dinner without them and have some mom and dad time. As a family, we talk, play cards, laugh, sit in a hot tub, swim, take long walks, hike, cook together, and just be with one another. This doesn't have to be expensive. We started these breaks going to state lodges or on camping trips, and as our finances grew, we turned them into more elaborate vacations at times. Once a year, we go away for 18 days, leaving on a Sunday afternoon and returning two and a half weeks later before the weekend. That gives us a break from the pastorate and our businesses and helps us to really appreciate our family, allowing us to gain a fresh perspective on life. We all need a two-week break once a year to truly detox and spend uninterrupted time with our families.

> Boundaries are to protect life, not to limit pleasures.
> EDWIN LOUIS COLE

We always attended church on the weekends except when we were out of town. We volunteered (and now work) in church as well. We learned to serve and had our children serve alongside us. I tried to volunteer where my children were as much as possible, so we could learn and minister side by side. As our schedules have grown busier and our family dynamics changed, we have had to adjust our schedules and systems to keep rebalancing our lives to the new demands. At one point, our home phone rang continuously with business, ministry, sales, and personal calls. It created a constant pressure that left no room for rest or family life. Finally, we saw the look of dread on our children's faces when it would ring, so a good friend suggested Gary make a voice message to direct the calls to the proper places. I still recall our long but necessary message to retrain business associates, church members, and ourselves to utilize the right channels before our personal life completely dissolved under the weight of responsibility. In a short time, calls were going to the right places, and our home returned to the refuge it should have been.

Boundaries

The woman who has "IT" has learned the importance of boundaries to help maintain balance and keep the urgent from stealing the important. All of us have days that don't turn out the way we intended, but if we have a system, the guidelines will help us stay on track in the overall scheme of life. I am not saying we should become inaccessible or say no all the time, but we do have to make sure the main goals of life are accomplished. Then there is time for the unexpected and spontaneous fun. I try to remember that I would not be where I am today if someone had not been willing to invest quality time in me, share parenting skills, bless me with a meal after becoming a new mommy, or encourage me with God's Word. To take an attitude of unwillingness to reach out to others is unacceptable; however, we have to do so with some boundaries and guidance. When Gary and I have failed to adhere to our priorities, which has happened on occasion, we gather the children together and apologize to them. We discuss the pitfalls, and, as a family, we put together workable solutions. Hopefully, this has modeled for our children how to talk out issues in life and work together for solutions.

Sometimes those solutions have come in the form of hiring out-side help or services for a period of time to accomplish certain tasks. There is nothing wrong with analyzing what you can or cannot manage in some seasons of life, and if the finances are available, getting the help you need to be able to stay focused on the highest priorities. Decades ago, new mothers (typically already staying at home) hired a diaper service to allow them time with their new baby. Today, women barely have any time before it's off to full-time work again.

When we were building our house, we couldn't manage the de--mands of business, ministry, homeschool, family, and...laundry! We found a local service that for $40 a week would wash, dry, and fold our clothes for a family of seven. To us, it was worth the money to have someone else handle this task so we could stay focused on priorities that were not as easily delegated. This worked for a season, but our strategies backfired occasionally! One time we bagged the laundry in separate large plastic bags for the laundry service, another couple bags for dry cleaning, and some added bags for Goodwill. We loaded them all into our van, positioning them systematically to be able to keep them apart. Somehow we mixed up the bags when dropping them off. Three days later, we picked up our dry cleaning and fresh clean laundry only to find out we had laundered all the Goodwill clothing and had given our regular clothes to Goodwill. Oops! After we got over the initial shock of losing our clothes, we had a good laugh as I examined what was left. In the future, I became more selective with what I gave to charity! Sometimes as Good Samaritans, we give away the ragged to "bless" others, but that time we gave our best (smile).

It's so important to me that we keep a merry heart in the midst of balancing the pressures of marriage, family, finances, work, and friends. I like the Scripture that says, *"He who is of a merry heart has a continual feast"* (Prov. 15:15). Stress and wrong attitudes can steal our ability to see the bright side in situations. It's not that we embrace the problem, but we need to trust God and be the virtuous woman who, because she provides for her loved ones spiritual food, clothing (even if

> **Make the Choice to Rejoice**
> AUTHOR UNKNOWN

it's lost at the Goodwill), and emotional strength, can laugh at the days ahead and sometimes at the days behind (see Prov. 31).

Adopt New Life Strategies

How many times do we let unrealistic expectations, overcommitment, or pressures from the demands of others create situations where we lose our perspective of the important. We can get so out of balance trying to please others that we stay wound up in knots and then unleash our frustration on those we love. I have had to learn the hard way to let go and trust God in situations that I can't change or that don't go the way I planned.

One such lesson came when we were getting ready for a Thanksgiving trip to Georgia. We were getting packed to leave with several small children, ages eight, six, and three, and I was pregnant with the fourth child. Talk about stress. We were running late; Gary had many loose ends to tie up in business, and I was frustrated that despite my plans and organization, we were not going to be on time. In the midst of leaving, Gary and I started playing the blame game. I thought he planned poorly, when in reality we both were overwhelmed with too much to do. My accusation left him aggravated, and we were both less than cordial as we started the long drive. I was trying to live up to others' expectations regarding the time we were to arrive, and I let that filter into stress and a lack of patience on my part.

Many hours of travel went by, and instead of our usual enjoyable road trip talks, I answered Gary's inquiries with short apathetic answers: "Where do you want to eat?" "I don't care." "Want to stop?" "Whatever you want." We went on like this for eight hours. After a traffic jam due to a car wreck in Chattanooga, I saw a stuffed animal on the wet pavement amidst broken glass and an overturned vehicle. A chill went through me as I thought about the possibility of a child in the terrible accident. I realized Gary and I were being foolish and giving "place to the devil" with our strife and unforgiving attitudes. Nevertheless, we kept moving down the highway. Either of us could have ended the silliness of this disagreement with a simple, "I'm sorry. Would you forgive me?" But we maintained our right to "be right" (which is almost always wrong).

Thirty minutes later, without warning, a 16-year-old young man pulled out in front of us on a two-lane highway, and we hit him broadside, sending our car into a spin. As our car spun out of control with heavy traffic in both lanes, I yelled, "Jesus! Jesus!" over and over. Everything seemed as though it was happening in slow motion. When our car stopped spinning, Gary and I met eyes, and in that brief moment we read each other's minds. Both of us turned slowly to see if our children were OK in the backseat. One began to gasp for air, and another had blood streaming down her face from a cut above her eye. Our three-year-old was missing, but crawled out from under a seat unharmed. After a few seconds, everyone reassured us they were OK. We all began to praise God spontaneously and then prayed for the young man who had hit us, and whose car was at the bottom of an embankment. We later learned that he was a pastor's son and was in rebellion against God.

Our strife and his rebellion opened the door to the enemy to do us all harm. After being transported to the hospital, I started having contractions, which eventually stopped as we prayed. Our son was kept in ICU overnight, but by the next day we were all released with scratches, bruises, and a few stitches. We can't afford to let strife enter our lives. "*He who has been born of God keeps himself, and the wicked one does not touch him*" (1 John 5:18 NKJV).

I often think God is unjustly blamed for problems and accidents, when in reality the door is opened through strife. I have learned if I am going to maintain my sanity, I must let go of my "perfect idea" and plan, releasing the need to control everything to be the way I expect it. It's a wonderful freedom to be released from the inner drive to perform to meet our own or others' expectations at the expense of our families.

I adopted some new life strategies after this experience. I was so grateful that we were all well and alive that I took on a new perspective. Gary and I would not allow strife between us or family members from that point forward. We would look at each other and say, "I'd rather prosper." To prosper is to be whole—spirit, soul, and body—and to have everything amply supplied in our lives. If we want to be whole in every way, we need to be balanced in priorities and keep the balance with joy. Stress and strife go hand in hand with being out of balance. Don't open the door to the devil by putting too many expectations on yourself or your spouse and family. Let it go quickly!

I found a sign that reads "Make the Choice to Rejoice" and hung it in our one small farmhouse bathroom. I hung it there because any time I would get stressed and start to feel as though I couldn't handle the pressure of the moment, I would go there to throw a pity party, but instead I would find my sign. It was my reminder to choose happiness, to choose God's joy instead of my problem. In my heart, I knew I would not leave the farmhouse until the work in me had been done and I could make right choices. The joy of the Lord is our strength, and the inner force of joy can keep us strong and laughing at the days to come. I moved out of the farmhouse, but the lessons I learned about rejoicing in trials and learning to balance our life priorities have stayed with me forever.

Get joyful about life! Laugh at things when they go wrong and refuse to let it get you down. The woman who has "IT" keeps choosing joy, and her life is a continual feast of laughter, peace, and balance.

get Results:
THE CONNECTION TO FAITH

Giving Birth to
Your Vision

The Power of
God's Word

Our Father Loves
to Give!

10 get Results:

THE CONNECTION TO FAITH

Through many dangers, toils, and snares,
I have already come...

John Newton

here is no dream without faith, and there is no faith without a fight! As I have watched one season after another unfold in my life, I can now look back with great awe as I see that everything I have believed God for in one way or another has or is coming to pass. There is no way that any of this could possibly be by coincidence or by sheer labor and tenacity.

I used to wonder what Jesus meant when He said, "*The kingdom of heaven suffers violence, and the violent take it by force*" (Matt. 11:12 NKJV). But with every victory of faith, I have learned there is a battle I must wage spiritually to win. Jesus has already purchased the victory on the cross, but I am responsible to know the truth, to live the truth, and to enforce it when circumstances try to rob me of its blessings. Jesus has already purchased the victory, but it is up to me to know the truth, to live the truth, and to enforce it when circumstances try to rob me of its blessings. Certainly we are in warfare, and there is a fight of faith that must be engaged to see God's Word and plan come to pass in this earth-cursed system, but there is a faith factor that has changed my life and destiny and will change yours as well.

Sometimes these fights are life or death. I have lost some battles, but I have not lost the war. One common denominator I have discovered in every battle is the pressure point—a defining moment that occurs on the brink of winning or falling backward. What we decide in that moment will dictate the final outcome. Even in the face of apparent defeat, I have seen God turn things around when I refused to let go of my belief in His Word. The bigger the reward or impact, the more intense the pressure, but I have also experienced the victory of following the still small voice of faith and releasing its power in the midst of pressure.

> We are locked in a battle. This is not a friendly, gentleman's discussion. It is a life and death conflict between the spiritual hosts of wickedness and those who claim the name of Christ.
>
> FRANCIS A. SCHAEFFER

Giving Birth to Your Vision

One area of my life where God has taught me a great deal about faith is in childbirth. I believe it goes back to the promise and calling God gave me concerning raising godly seed (children). The principles I learned are the same ones you need to know if you are "pregnant" with a vision—a dream God has placed inside of you that you know you are to bring into the earth. We carry a vision, then we wait on it to come to pass. We go through transitions, changes, pressures, and then one day, if we have fed and protected it properly, we give birth and see before us everything we labored over for so long.

While I was pregnant with our first child, I had prayed for nine months that God would envelop my baby and protect her spirit, soul, and body and give me a wonderful delivery with no medications, intervention, or complications. My doctor knew my wishes and had agreed to let me do whatever I wanted in the delivery. I wanted my baby alert when she was born, and I wanted to fully enjoy every moment of the experience. I labored 13 hours and was handling it well, but then the doctor informed me that my labor was not progressing quickly enough and soon they would need to operate. (I have since been involved in 36 births and have heard this told to many other women.)

Weary from labor, my confidence had already been shaken, and I knew I was on the precipice of letting go of my faith as well. In that moment, I shut my eyes and said, "God, help me. Have mercy on me and help me hold on to my faith." I had just finished praying in between contractions when a spiritual leader in my life walked through the door of the room. Immediately the Spirit of God leapt in me, and I felt a wave of encouragement. We prayed, and I started to boldly speak the Word of God that I had declared over my pregnancy from the beginning. As I did, almost without thought, I told my body to obey that Word of God and finish the labor and delivery, as I had believed all along. I can't describe how it happened, but immediately a confidence in God and His promise superseded the negative circumstances and pressure I had experienced. Within minutes, my labor began to accelerate the dilation. I delivered a beautiful, healthy baby girl just as I had prayed. The battle had been intense, but the victory was sweet as I looked into the eyes of wonder of our newborn daughter.

I came to understand the connection between the Word of God and my enforcement of it through my heart belief and declaration. Jesus said, "*Have faith in God. I tell you the truth, if anyone [I am just naive enough to believe that means anyone] says to this mountain, 'Go throw yourself in the sea,' and does not doubt in his heart but believes what he says will happen, it will be done for him. …Whatever you ask for in prayer, believe that you have received it, and it will be yours*" (Mark 11:22–24, bracketed copy mine). Notice it says to believe you "have received" it. Faith has a picture of the request as already done. Faith is the substance—the thing it is produced from—of what we hope for and the evidence of what we do not see (see Heb. 11:1). Our faith actually brings into reality the thing for which we hope.

How do we get faith? Faith comes into our heart by the Word of God (see Rom. 10:8). As I see the picture that God's Word paints for me, I envision what I hope for as done. The more I listen to God's voice (His Word), the easier it is for my heart to believe and receive what He says is truth. This principle is the foundation of faith in the Kingdom of God and the way Jesus operated God's Kingdom in the earth. It is also His example to us of how we are to live in His Kingdom. The just shall live by faith (see Rom. 1:17), and anyone who comes to God must believe that He is and that He is a rewarder of those who diligently seek Him (see Heb. 11:6). Through faith, God framed the world by speaking creation into existence. God said, "Let there be...," and everything we see came into being. God envisioned it through the eyes of faith and spoke it into existence. Faith is substance.

> God's Word is pure and sure, in spite of the devil, in spite of your fear, in spite of everything.
>
> R. A. TORREY

Each of my childbirth experiences has had its own set of unique circumstances, and I have grown with each one to understand the power of God's Word and spiritual laws of the Kingdom. During the second birth I had to push for a long time and wanted to quit at that stage, but God's grace gave me the ability to push through tiredness and hold the vision in my hand of a strong healthy son. To see our dreams come to pass, we are oftentimes going to feel as though we can't make it or that it's too hard. But we must push on. We can do it!

The Power of God's Word

The greatest battle I faced in childbirth came while Gary and I were preparing to go to the next level in the plan of God. I was cleaning the rental home we had occupied for the previous year and making the last preparations for our move from Oklahoma to Ohio. As I cleaned that day, I reflected back on how we had stood on the Word of God concerning the sale of the house we owned before renting. The housing market had collapsed in our city's oil-based economy, and our house had been worth less than we owed on it. One morning I read the Scripture, "*And everyone who has left houses or brothers or sisters or father or mother or children or fields for My sake will receive a hundred times as much and will inherit eternal life*" (Matt. 19:29). At the time, I knew I needed to let go of the house and believe God to sell it so we could be free to carry out God's plan for our lives.

The house had been on the market for many months, and there had not been one showing. I began to pray over the house and literally gave it to God, then I declared it "Sold." That week I contacted the Realtor and asked to be released from the contract so I could sell it myself. The Realtor agreed. Then we went to the bank and explained that we owed more on it than it was worth. The loan officer quickly said, "We have a stack of foreclosures and don't want another one! If you can find a buyer for this house, we will take an offer for whatever it appraises. But good luck finding a buyer in this market." After getting the adjusted appraisal price, we ran an ad in the newspaper, which I carefully crafted and prayed over. We held an open house over the weekend, and by Monday, I had an offer and the house was sold.

With that great memory of God's faithfulness a year previous, I anticipated the new journey ahead, as we now prepared to move to accomplish our "end-time work" in Ohio. That day, an exterminator came in and sprayed for fleas brought in from a couple of cocker spaniel puppies we had gotten for the children. Within a short time of his leaving, I began to feel sick, but I thought maybe it was just a pregnancy sickness. A friend picked me up to go and hang wallpaper at her house. As she drove, I began to hallucinate and cry. I was overwhelmed by fear and actually thought someone was after me. I remember seeing a mail truck and asking my friend why the police were after me! I have never used drugs in my life, but this was the closest thing I could imagine to a bad drug trip. As she walked me into her house, my friend knew something was severely wrong. I lay on her couch crying and declaring, "God will never leave me nor forsake me," over and over. I barely knew what I was doing or what was happening. My husband came for me, and by the time he arrived, I started to become more coherent.

Trying to figure out what had happened, we called the exterminator and asked about the chemicals he sprayed in our rental house and the reaction I had. He admitted that he was not licensed for extermination and that he had sprayed *termite* chemicals in the house! Realizing our unborn child had been exposed to the chemicals, we prayed over our child and tried to keep fear out of our thoughts. I wrote many Scriptures on paper and hung them on the ceiling of our bedroom. I would lie in bed and read them out loud.

One morning I woke up and a particular Scripture seemed to jump off the ceiling at me. *"Death and life are in the power of the tongue, and those who love it will eat its fruit"* (Prov. 18:21 NKJV). When I went to get up, I realized I was bleeding and had symptoms of miscarriage. I began to pray and sensed the Spirit of God in me so clearly say, "Don't surround yourself with doubt and unbelief." Gary was away on a business day trip, so I called a mature Christian friend and told her what was happening. She said, *"This child shall live and not die and declare the works of the Lord"* (based on Psalm 118:17). Then she came and drove me to a faith-based hospital in our city.

I held tight to the words concerning life and death being in the power of my tongue (my words), and that I had to fight with spiritual weapons—my words could unleash life or death. I chose life. By faith I began to thank God that my child was fine and that it was well. I remembered the Shunammite woman, who after she found her son was dead still said, "IT is well," when Elisha's servant inquired of her (see 2 Kings 4:26 NKJV). And she received her son back to life, *"the God who gives life to the dead and calls things that are not as though they were"* (Rom. 4:17).

I had never been in a fight like this, but I was so glad my heart had been prepared in God's Word. When fear tried to hold me captive and get me to hand over my child's life, faith was there to answer. The woman who gets "IT" learns to align her heart and her words with God's Word and His heart. She speaks words that bring life into every situation.

The doctor came in the room and without examining me said, "This child shall live and not die and declare the works of God." I almost leapt off the table! Only God could have given him those words. As my friend and I had done, this doctor spoke life over my child instead of the normal medical protocol. He never said the words miscarriage to me, even though the bleeding and cramping I was experiencing was significant. He encouraged me to stand in faith. I asked him what I should do, and he said to just act normal and trust God. Oh, if more doctors had a knowledge of God and His power! Over the next two days, I bled as if having a miscarriage, but I continued to say the words, "My child shall live and not die and declare the works of God." The bleeding stopped, and I continued to full term.

Just weeks before I delivered, I was in a church service praying over my unborn baby. There were days, such as this one, when thoughts would try to hit me that something was going to be wrong with my baby. We had already been through two severe attacks and had made a major move across country while I was seven months' pregnant. On this morning, as I prayed I thought of Elijah the prophet, and how Elisha had asked God for a double portion of Elijah's blessing (see 2 Kings 2:9). I knew in that moment that God was answering me with a promise, as He always does. I asked God for my child to have a double portion of God's blessing, and I received it for my child. The minister got up to preach, and his sermon was about Elijah and Elisha and the double portion. I rejoiced. Weeks later, our son was born healthy and whole. We named him Thomas, after his grandfather, and later found a plaque in a bookstore that read, "Thomas, meaning: double portion." Today, he is declaring the Word of God.

The next two children's births were easy, and it seemed as though we sailed through them without much pressure at all. With our last child, Kirsten, I never felt a single contraction and literally delivered her after a party in our home with no pain. It was a celebration! That seems to parallel our lives and vision. The first battle we encounter may be tough to break through, but as we grow in God and His Word, we get stronger and more confident that "*everything is possible for him who believes*" (Mark 9:23).

Years later the same simple principles of faith have brought tremendous blessings to our lives, and we have learned that we can always rely on God's Kingdom laws. Just as we are confident in physical laws such as gravity, the laws of the Kingdom can be learned, and as we confidently apply them to our lives, we can prevail in adversity. We

> Open your hearts to the love God instills. God loves you tenderly. What He gives you is not to be kept under lock and key but to be shared.
> MOTHER TERESA

will always face battles as long as we are in this earth, but faith overcomes. The woman who has "IT" understands that through faith and patience she will inherit the promises of God, so she doesn't quit in the heat of the battle or blame God, but rather she becomes a skillful warrior.

Our Father Loves to Give!

People limit their dreams to what they see as possibilities. If you don't think it is possible, you won't let yourself dream about it. That's why the role of faith is so important, because literally, "Everything is possible for him who believes." Faith removes our limitations and lets us see visions far beyond our background, our upbringing, or our resources.

Gary and I have started several very successful businesses, a wonderful church, and built a family and entire life on the principles of faith. We haven't always gotten it all right, but we learn from our mistakes. Faith—it's the only way to live!

In our business, many vendors offer incentive trips, and because I love to travel, especially free trips, I enjoy winning them. On one occasion, a trip to England was offered by one of our vendors. From the beginning, I prayed that we would receive the trip, and I believed, thanking God for it throughout the duration of the contest. We told our regional director that we were going. But because we were so busy with the ministry, Gary did not have enough time to invest in business to win the contest and we fell short. However, when you have believed something for so long (it had been almost a year since the contest's beginning), you just don't accept defeat. It was so formed in my thinking and belief system that I couldn't let go and accept we hadn't won. A month went by, and I never once said, "We didn't win."

One day we received a call from our regional director. "You are not going to believe this. The company just called me and had a few openings for the trip, which they offered to you and me, because I am your director. I know you prayed for this, and if you hadn't, my wife and I wouldn't be going, so we want to take an early excursion with you to Scotland as well." Not only did we win the trip to England, we went to Scotland, too. That's what I call "*exceedingly abundantly above all that we ask or think, according to the power that works in us*" (Eph. 3:20 NKJV). As we toured beautiful castles and enjoyed the seaside cliffs, I thanked God for His principle of faith and His great love to share with us the beauty of His creation.

The woman who gets "IT" doesn't quit! Don't cast away your confidence because it has a mighty reward, that after you have done the will of God, you will receive the promise of God (see Heb. 10:35–36).

As we have endeavored to follow God, He expands our vision to do things that appear impossible. If it's something that we can do in ourselves, it's rarely big enough to be a vision from God. He always calls us to do things that we can only accomplish with His Word and faith. We start learning in the small things that are opportunities to grow so we are able to use faith in the bigger battles and come out with the victor's crown. One day we are going to receive *"the crown of life that God has promised to those who love Him"* (James 1:12). The reward I most want to receive is to hear Jesus say, *"Well done, good and faithful servant; you were faithful over a few things, I will make you ruler over many things. Enter into the joy of your lord"* (Matt. 25:21 NKJV). That's a contest I don't plan to miss.

The woman who gets "IT" seizes the day by faith with eternity's vision in her windshield and God's goodness and mercy in her rearview mirror.

I love how one of Jesus' closest disciples asked Him, *"We have left everything to follow You! What then will there be for us?"* (Matt. 19:27). God never gets offended that we want or ask to receive. All children do! Our children were always asking us for things, and we enjoyed giving them. People may get bothered. Religion definitely gets bothered, but Father God doesn't. He holds out rewards to us throughout the Scriptures. I wish people knew just how good He is and that following Him brings great reward in every part of our lives. Religion has chased so many people away from God by making Him seem like a hard, angry God instead of the loving Father He really is. Jesus answered Peter's request by saying (my paraphrase), "No one has left basically anything for Me that she will not receive hundreds of times more in this life and eternal life to come." You can't beat that.

The woman who gets "IT" receives the best reward!

get Dreams:

PAST OBSTACLES AND MOVING FORWARD

God Is a God of Restoration

Seize the Moment

Be Patient With Your Aspirations

Change Your Thinking

You Can Do It

11
get Dreams:

PAST OBSTACLES
AND MOVING
FORWARD

One of the most tragic things I know about human nature is that all of us tend to put off living. We are all dreaming of some magical rose garden over the horizon instead of enjoying the roses that are blooming outside our windows today.

Dale Carnegie

Inside every woman, hidden secrets are locked away—secrets from the past, secret dreams for today, and secret desires for her future and family. For far too many women, these secrets remain just that. When they take steps toward their dreams, a little voice inside says, "You could never do that." "You don't deserve to have happiness." "Look at all the mistakes you've made." "You've been through a divorce, which disqualifies you from your dreams." What blocks the way may even be there because of a decision that was out of her control or something someone else did to her that was unfair and unjustified. We've already talked about forgiveness and the freedom that comes when we forgive others. But we also need to let go of the guilt, shame, and the lack of confidence associated with mistakes or regrets.

The debilitating force of rehearsing the past and living with regret can hold us hostage and keep us from moving forward. It robs us of the confidence to take the necessary chances in life that help us grow and accomplish the impossible. Many women are waiting on God to do something for them, when He is waiting on them to do something! I don't mean that we should act on foolish whims, but we must be willing to take some calculated inspired risks to reach our destiny.

I spoke with a friend who grew up without positive role models or teaching from God's Word concerning marriage, and who out of insecurity and the desire to escape her home life married an abusive man. When the marriage failed because it was based on a faulty foundation, she said it was as though a big scarlet letter "D" for divorce was emblazoned across her forehead. Religious people condemned her, and she felt alienated from God and rejected. But once she gained an understanding of the love and grace of her heavenly Father, she was able to forgive the past and herself, renewing her dreams and moving forward. Today she has a wonderful marriage and family, and she is working to make a difference in the life of a young woman who was abandoned by her family.

> Dreams are renewable. No matter what our age or condition, there are still untapped possibilities within us and new beauty waiting to be born.
> DALE E. TURNER

God Is a God of Restoration

My intent in this book is to help women get God's big picture for their lives and encourage them to seek God's specific blueprint for how He wants to help build their dreams as they help others. I call it: *Live IT! Give IT!*

It is all too easy for us to give up on God's plan when we have experienced personal setbacks or someone failed to live up to their part of the plan. When this happens, God often gets the blame and His ways are considered faulty. We shouldn't fault the Creator when plans don't go the way we hoped, but instead we need to recognize the real enemy and the frailty of human beings and their decisions. We have all made mistakes!

For instance, God's plan for marriage works when both parties agree to build their marriage around His foundation. If a husband rebels against God, a wife cannot make him obey God. She needs to remain faithful to God and love her husband in every way she can and pray for him without ceasing, but God's love allows for choice, both right and wrong, and she can't save what he rejects. God is always faithful to this woman as she seeks Him, even if her husband is not.

I know a beautiful woman who committed her time and life to be a stay-at-home mother, as she and her husband agreed was best. She admitted that the marriage started on a rocky foundation, but she had accepted most of the blame for the problems in the home. She had very low self-esteem and did not command respect in the way she presented herself or allowed herself to be treated by her husband (usually children will treat their mother the way they see their father treat her). She existed on antidepressants and coped with her "shame" by being everyone's doormat.

Once she made a decision to stop medicating her low self-esteem, she began to apply many of the principles concerning freedom discussed in the "Get Freedom" chapter. She started to realize how much God loves her and that she is valuable and precious to Him. He became her God, first and foremost, her first love, and as she received His love for her, she found she could truly love others. That love changed everything for her.

Here's why. With love, there must also be respect. Jesus said, *"If you love Me, you will obey what I command"* (John 14:15). True love requires respect or corresponding action. If we do not respect ourselves, others will not as well. We cannot be a doormat or take false responsibility for others' decisions. I have counseled many women who have allowed their children or husband to manipulate them with guilt, shame, and abuse to get what they wanted and shirk their responsibility for problems. God's love demands that we do not live in a prison of pain, blame, or shame.

When this woman came off the antidepressants, she realized that not everything that had happened was her fault, and the blame her husband so readily heaped upon her was not solely her responsibility. His late night hours at work and unwillingness to account for why he did not come home some nights led her to question his behavior and account for his choices. He responded by telling her to get back on the medication.

Realizing he was involved with another woman, over a period of time she got the courage to confront him. She let him know that although she loved him, she expected change in his behavior if he wanted to keep their marriage. Thinking she didn't have the inner strength to do anything about it, he refused to accept any responsibility or to make changes. After another extended time of him not coming home for many nights, she put her foot down and said, "I love you, but I will not be treated this way. Either we go to counseling and you commit to make our marriage work, or move out. Enough is enough!" He chose to move out.

She had never had this kind of self-respect until she accepted God's love for her and understood it was not right to be treated this way. For her sake and her children, she refused to condescend to live in humiliation and degradation again. Realizing that her children would adopt the same attitudes she allowed to be played out in their marriage, she was motivated to fight for their protection and to get the spiritual and legal counsel she needed. Her church family supported her in prayer with understanding and kept her strong emotionally.

For the first time in her married life, she worked to provide for her children, assisting with housekeeping in the church. She remained prayerful for her husband, hoping he would change his heart and return with a right commitment, and God provided for her and her children. Almost a year later, he filed for a divorce, which she did not agree to initially, but after two and a half years of waiting, praying, and working, God spoke in her heart that it was over. She was released from waiting any longer. By this time, she had grown into a woman who knew who she was in Christ and had learned to accept that she was worthy of love. I remember sharing with her that as I prayed, God told me He had a prince for her, but He wanted to be a Prince to her until then.

She had grown so close to God through these difficulties that she was no longer weak and codependent, but had become a stronger daughter of God who realized her value and beauty. And one day God brought her a prince as well. A wonderful man came into her life and became a great encouragement and leader to her and the children. She did not leave God's plans for her life behind in her earlier desperation, but God restored the desires of her heart as she grew in His love to a deeper level.

Today her understanding of God's goodness and faithfulness is so evident. She said, "During the separation and divorce, I had to make sure my children knew that it was not God's plan or

> Your past is not your potential. In any hour you can choose to liberate the future.
>
> MARILYN FERGUSON

His Word that failed. It was the bad choices people made." She and her husband are currently ministering and bringing restoration to brokenhearted people, and her children are actively involved in ministry, following God's plan as a family together. She says, "It's not because I was the perfect mother, but because God is a perfect Father. He was there for me and my children when their dad wasn't."

God is all about restoration. The woman who has "IT" lets go of the past but doesn't let go of God's Word or plan because of her circumstances.

Seize the Moment

In every season of life, there are new possibilities. My passion is that every woman would savor the wonderful opportunities and joys of each life season without looking back with regret or looking ahead with such anticipation that she misses the beauty of the season she has now been given. Every part of our lives is a window of opportunity, whether it's going to college, experiencing singleness or marriage, raising children, building a business or career, ministering, grandparenting, or exiting this life into our eternal rewards. If we fail to seize the moment and enjoy the unique opportunities each season of our lives affords, we will possibly linger in regret or miss out on this day, dreading what we have to do.

We cannot navigate forward while we are looking backward, and we can't worry enough to change tomorrow in a positive way. But worry can take years away from our lives and undermine our health. Many illnesses and diseases stem from emotional cancers and cares. Jesus instructed us, *"Do not worry about tomorrow, for tomorrow will worry about itself. Each day has enough trouble of its own"* (Matt. 6:34). It's not that we don't plan or dream, but we can't be anxious about tomorrow and miss today. God has a way of bringing everything in its season, especially if we are making the best decisions we can in the season in which we are living. I want to see women live "IT" today. Once we live "IT," we can give "IT"!

Just because we have faced some obstacles or hurdles in life, we shouldn't throw out God's plan! The woman who has "IT" is constantly growing and learning and letting God's Word define and reinvent her through every season of life.

When I was a young woman, there was a time when I wanted to be older so I would be taken seriously; then one day I woke up and thought I was too old to make a difference. I decided to get busy helping youth and tried to offer them the spiritual guidance I desired as a younger woman. That opened an entire new world to me as I poured myself into their lives. I grew and changed as I found a meaningful purpose to release my time and energy into that made a difference. I loved them, and they reciprocated. I am convinced that we are never too young or old to make an impact. We just need to look for opportunities and act on them!

A strong belief exists in our society that everything of value is built around youth, and that older age is a negative downhill experience. The cultural importance of youth and beauty, as defined by today's images of sexuality and changing propaganda, can leave mature women feeling as though they don't have "IT" anymore. If we believe these lies, they become self-fulfilling prophecies. Instead, we should see this as a season of enjoying the fruits of our labor and imparting wisdom and guidance into the next generation. I want to shout it from the rooftops that many of the women who have "IT" in the greatest way are over 50! I like to say, "She's STILL got it!"

The negative outlook on older age is a relatively new attitude. Throughout history, wisdom from elders was honored and upheld as a position of respect. The older women were to teach the younger (see Titus 2:2–3). In this way, womanhood was honored and timeless principles were preserved, as well as the arts of homemaking, child rearing, and understanding marriage. According to the Word of God, gray hair is a crown of glory and wisdom (see Prov. 16:31), and we have lost this guidance. Our expectation should be that as we grow in wisdom, we have more to offer, greater things to give. The Scriptures encourage us that *"those who hope in the Lord will renew their strength. They will soar on wings like eagles; they will run and not grow weary, they will walk and not be faint"* (Isa. 40:31). We don't have to faint as we grow in age; instead, we can run!

> It is impossible to win the race unless you venture to run; impossible to win the victory unless you dare to battle.
>
> RICHARD DEVOS

Some of my favorite women who've "still got it" are doing amazing things to bring joy and wisdom into the lives of so many others. One of these ladies, who is over 75 years old, pastors a prominent church with her husband and mentors women like me. The other is in her eighties, lives on her own, serves God, taking care of children in the nursery, and brings a smile to everyone with whom she comes in contact! She's even been known to help toilet paper the yards of others who are retiring from their careers. Every weekend I personally look forward to seeing her precious face, lined with wisdom, as beautiful as a doll, and the warm hug she always gives me. People will say of the woman who grows in maturity and maintains a positive attitude, "She's still got IT."

Instead of viewing our lives with negativity because we face challenges, we need to see those obstacles as opportunities. Scripture instructs us to "*fight the good fight of the faith*" (1 Tim. 6:12). It is a fight! It's not flesh and blood we are fighting against, but we do face situations in life that can challenge us to the core of our being. When challenged or tempted, we should never think that God is causing the problem, but instead see Him as the answer. God's plan is perfect, but our execution isn't! Many times I have made mistakes or thought I had the right direction in a situation only to find out I didn't have a clear understanding and had things I needed to learn. There have also been times I had clear direction, but lacked the discipline to act on it and see it through. Our Father wants to continue to mentor and train us by His Spirit so we can run our race and make it to the finish line. We're never too old to keep learning.

Be Patient With Your Aspirations

During our children's formative years, I had made a commitment to be a stay-at-home mom. Finances were tight during those days, and we were living in the 1800's farmhouse. One day I received a call from a female financial advisor who had contacted my husband about opening an office for their corporation in our town. She was looking for someone to run the agency franchise and wanted referrals. Gary thought I might know someone and directed her to me. As we talked, she began to tell me what a lucrative opportunity it was. Before we finished our conversation, she talked me into meeting with her and taking their company test and profile.

A week after our meeting, she called with great enthusiasm about me opening the office for their corporation. I was hesitant, but also greatly flattered as she told me she had never had anyone score as highly on their test, and that the president wanted to meet me the next morning and hire me on the spot, pending my interview. *My world was rocked.* I had gone along with this process almost innocently, and now I was on the verge of a major decision! What to do?

I put together my best corporate outfit. My role had been to work with my husband in our businesses, but he was the primary, and I was the vice president of whatever needed to be done. This was an opportunity to have a business that was mine. I thought about the ramifications for the children, our marriage, and on the partnership Gary and I had formed from the beginning as one team. As I lay in bed that evening nervously contemplating these things, I felt uneasy but excited at the same time. I prayed, "God, You know how feisty and strong-willed I can be. If this isn't Your will, don't speak gently to me. Hit me over the head with a two-by-four if this is not Your plan." I'm sure there was already doubt in my heart, or I wouldn't have prayed this way.

The next morning I inspected myself from head to toe and looked very professional and tailored—every hair in place, stilettos, and briefcase. I kissed my family goodbye. I shut the door on all the activity in the house and climbed into our family Caravan, being careful to keep the snow off my patent pumps. As I navigated down the long driveway, my tires slipped and

I went off the driveway and came to a halt in the deep snow. The harder I pressed the accelerator, the deeper my tires went. I couldn't even climb out of the vehicle with the foot of snow on the ground. Gary came out and tried to dislodge the tires with boards, but to no avail. Frustrated and full of anxiety, I said to him, "You don't want me to get that position, do you? I knew it!" What does a guy say in a moment like that? I chuckle now to think about it. That day it seemed so important! Gary had remained neutral, knowing that I had to decide this one for myself, or I would forever feel as though someone trapped me into being a "keeper at home."

I called the neighbor across the street and asked to borrow her car. All she had was an old pickup, since her husband had their car. I walked our long driveway, trying to keep my feet dry, and went to her front door. Keys in hand, I tried to start her pickup. The engine turned over and over, but after 15 minutes it was flooded and still no success. The neighbor invited me into her home. Realizing I was upset, she said, "What are you doing that is so important, Drenda?" I told her the story. I needed to call the company and attempt to reschedule the appointment. But before I could, this woman, who had raised two children herself and now had an empty nest, said to me, "Drenda, what are you doing? Your husband and children need you! You can never go back and get this time back with your family." That was the two-by-four I needed. She was right, and I knew it. There would be opportunities to be a businesswoman later, but my present season of opportunities would never return.

> At the end of your life, you will never regret not having passed one more test, not winning one more verdict or not closing one more deal. You will regret time not spent with a husband, a friend, a child, or a parent.
> BARBARA BUSH

I called the company female executive and explained that I didn't think the position was for me. She tried to convince me I was overreacting to a rough morning and encouraged me to not shut the door. I knew better. It had been a rough morning, but it was clear where my priorities needed to be for this season. She continued to call me once a week for a month, but I never relented. Months later, the office opened, and a few times I drove past it and thought, *What if?* Three years later, it closed, but mine and Gary's business flourished and so did our children.

Change Your Thinking

Dreams are God's language, and He invites each of us to dream again. Take care of your health, your emotional and physical well-being, and nurture your dreams, not through demands and temper tantrums, but through seeking God first and letting His Kingdom make a way where there seems to be impossibility. Your Father knows how to touch your heart with intimate and hand-tailored blessings when no one else may know your secret pain or your shattered dreams. God will put the pieces back together if you will let Him. It will take courage and requires faith. But He will give you the courage to step out when you must make a tough decision or to step up when it's time to let your light shine in the darkness. There is so much potential in every woman, especially when she gives herself wholeheartedly to the plans of God. "'*I know the plans I have for you,' declares the Lord, 'plans to prosper you and not to harm you, plans to give you hope and a future*'" (Jer. 29:11).

I have written my dreams down in the form of goals and thoughts for many years. As each of those dreams came to pass, I found that they gave way to new visions and dreams. As I accomplished a new goal, its reach gave me a new vantage point, and I could see the next mountain to climb. By just starting to climb with a dream in front of me, it continually stretched me to the next level of growth.

We should always be improving ourselves. I refuse to settle, to quit, or to back down. Everything we desire is not going to come easily or without some effort and change. Change is never comfortable, but the results are worth it! One of the beautiful traits of women is our adaptability to situations, but sometimes we adapt to cope with negative situations or crises and then park there. Our mindsets and corresponding action become stuck, and we need to change to move forward.

After managing our tight family budget for many years, I had adjusted to living very frugally and had placed many of my needs on the back burner. As we came out of debt, I still had many leftover attitudes about money, and so did Gary. We had learned the evils of debt, but God began to teach us about His abundant care and desire to bless us as well. This was still a struggle for us.

Since I had traveled abroad as a young girl, I had dreamed of going back to Paris, but this time with Gary. We had managed to pay off our debts, but we still had a lot of things we needed. I had a big birthday coming in four months, so I began to drop hints to Gary about going to Paris. As the weeks passed and there was no movement on his part to get passports or make travel plans, I knew my scheme was doomed. I was disappointed and began to feel a little sorry for myself.

On my birthday, Gary came home and said, "Grab some clothes. We're going overnight somewhere." As we drove, I gave myself a mental pep talk. "Whatever he does, Drenda, be appreciative. Your relationship is more important than anything he does or doesn't do." As we drove toward the city, I thought perhaps he was going to fly me to see my parents in Georgia. But he pulled into a local mall and said he wanted to buy me an outfit, and money was no object. I thought, *Oh well, we can go to that new store, Nordstroms.*

Neither of us had been in Nordstroms before, and as we ascended the second floor escalator, I spied a beautiful pink and black suit in view. Both of us felt out of place as the store attendant showed us the suit. I had trained myself to look at the price tag before I would even consider any purchase. When we both saw the price, we were shocked and quickly but graciously left the store.

Walking around other mall stores, I tried to find something on sale that would work, but didn't see anything I liked. Finally, Gary turned to me and said, "Drenda, for all the years you have put everyone else above your own needs, I don't care what that outfit cost. I'm going to buy it for you!" We went back to Nordstroms, and he told the attendant to fix me up head to toe, not only with the suit but shoes, hosiery, and jewelry. To my embarrassment, I was actually wearing Gary's socks, because I had gotten in a habit of sharing them to save money! I took off my rags and disposed of my husband's socks in the ladies room. I had never tried on a $2,000 outfit before, and I felt like Cinderella as I wore the stunning suit from the store, with several clerks following me to the door. Remarkably, the suit was actually called "Parisian Pink."

We left and drove toward a small college town, where as a perceptive female I knew Gary was taking me to an English-style

lodge we had stayed at before. I had my new outfit and anticipated enjoying a quiet dinner with Gary. Much to my surprise,
as we walked into a hallway, Gary flung open a door and led
me into an elegantly decorated candlelit room filled with 75 or
more of my friends, church members, and family. I cried for the
next hours as Gary, friends, and family toasted me, our children
sang to me, and I opened cards and gifts. Now I really felt like
Cinderella at the ball. Gary said, "I know you mentioned going
to Paris, but I had already planned this and felt God told me to
do this for you to show you His love."

Something changed in me that night. Every family, career, or financial sacrifice made seemed as nothing compared to the great
joy of this evening. I also felt the great care of God's love and
knew that He wanted to bless me with good things. This involved a significant mindset change. I was still willing to make
sacrifices, but I didn't need to let the past financial struggle hold
me in a mental grip anymore. If I could receive from God at
the Goodwill (as I had many times in the past), why couldn't I
receive from a nice department store as well? I learned that God
wasn't limited unless I limited Him. And
we even ended up in Paris and much of Europe with our entire family three years later.

I needed to change my thinking. It had been
necessary to live frugally for a season, but I
had settled for it as a way of life. Don't get
me wrong: I still love a bargain, an auction,

> The greatest discovery
> of my generation is
> that you can change
> your circumstances by
> changing your attitudes
> of mind.
> WILLIAM JAMES

or a sale, but I don't have to limit God. I love to make my children laugh and to bless them with good things, and God wants
to give good gifts to His children, and they're not all "spiritual"
as we may rationalize. We've all met someone who lived through

the Great Depression and fears spending money. I once knew an elderly lady who wore tattered gloves, so I bought her a new pair for Christmas. She took me to her dresser and placed them neatly in the drawer along with six other pair of brand-new gloves. She couldn't use or enjoy them because she was stuck in the Depression. She also kept every piece of twine, bread ties, ribbon, bags, paper, and cellophane!

Yesterday may be history, but if we aren't careful, we will let it hold us in misery today.

You Can Do It

Ask yourself what behaviors, habits, and old patterns of thinking and acting are holding you back from being the best person you can be, living the best life you can live, and giving the world your individualized "special brand" uniquely designed by God. When was the last time you changed your hairstyle or bought a new outfit? Are you letting uncontrolled spending hold you in a prison of debt? Are you letting codependent relationships steal your future? Stop it. You are not a victim. God wants you to take care of others *and* to take care of yourself. If you do not invest into your health, fitness, presentation, and well-being (spirit, soul, and body), you won't have much to offer others, and what you do offer may turn others away. We must have enough self-value to see that we are worth the investment that Jesus made to bring us into the Kingdom.

I have seen women who were unwilling to make the sacrifices the current season of life required, which only caused them to be denied of future blessings. Their self-centered attitudes and reckless spending habits caused them to miss future joys, because they could not discipline themselves to delay the rewards and gratification until the right time. I have also seen women who couldn't receive the rewards of enjoying their labors when the payoff came. Let's not be either of these!

In our family, our daughter Polly has struggled with weight since she was eight years old. I always thought it was my fault, since I bribed her with candy during the potty-training years. She would sit on the potty, holding her little hand out and asking for more "din-din" (candy). Anything to get her to go! Each year she gained a little more weight, which I attributed to our busier lifestyle and eating out more often versus the first three children who were raised more on home-cooked meals and smaller portions. By the time she was 16, she was 50 pounds overweight. I tried to encourage her to make different meal choices, while trying not to damage her self-esteem in the process. It was so difficult to shop for her and find fashionable clothing in her size. It made us both sad and usually shopping ended with her in tears and me trying to encourage her, holding back mine.

One morning she woke up and told me she was going to lose weight, and this time she was going to do it with God's help. She said, "My Scripture is, *I can do all things through Christ who strengthens me*" (Phil. 4:13). Over a year's time of exercising and changing her habits, she lost almost 65 pounds. Today, she is very healthy and whole, and she learned that she can change her life with God's help. And so can you!

Many of us are waiting for someone else to say, "You can do it!" We wait for someone to acknowledge our unique ability and bring us into the light. We all know in our hearts that we were created for something special. Everyone wants to feel special, to be somebody we are proud of, and to accomplish something worthwhile. Unfortunately, we may not have a circle of cheerers or supporters, but be assured, God is always speaking words of encouragement. When you fall down and skin your knee, He knows how to help you get back up, mend the bruises, and He says, "You're not going down. Make some adjustments and keep moving forward! I believe in you."

We will never get it perfect, no matter how hard we work or how completely we endeavor to follow God's plans. That's why we need "IT"; that's why we need Him. But if we keep moving forward, we will ultimately arrive much further than we ever dreamed possible when we were stuck. And the blessings will far outweigh the price.

"IT"

What is "IT"? As Jesus hung on the cross in His last moments of agony, He spoke the words, *"IT is finished"* (John 19:30). "IT" is the reason He came—to give His life for you. "IT" is the restoration He purchased. Through His pain and suffering He paid the price for all of humanity's sin. Every pain, every problem, and every dysfunction that entered the face of the earth as a curse when Adam and Eve opened Pandora's box through disobedience was paid for on that day. "IT" includes everything we need in life. "IT" changed everything forever.

The woman who has "IT" has everything she needs for life and godliness. When she realizes she already has been given "IT," it is simply a matter of learning what has been given to her. She has restoration. She has answers to life's toughest challenges. Because she has "IT," she can hold her head high and laugh at the days to come. She doesn't have to be caught off guard. She doesn't have to live a life of defeat. She has the Holy Spirit to guide her into all truth (see John 16:13). He will be her teacher. His will shall be done on earth as it is in Heaven. His will is His Word. When Jesus faced a challenge from the enemy, He answered it with, *"IT is written"* (Matt. 4:4). "IT" is the Word of God. Jesus is the Word of God who came in the flesh (see John 1:14). When we see Jesus, we see "IT IS FINISHED."

The only thing that stands between her and the restoration of all things in her life is simply knowing the truths from the Word of God. Once she knows these truths, she can enact the plan of God in every area of her life. "IT" works! If she's been broken, there is healing. If she has lacked, there is abundant supply. If she is sad, there is joy. If she has been disillusioned in any area of life, God's Word will produce a new vision, a new picture of hope for her faith to believe in. She can be all that she was created to be.

She receives "IT" by faith in God's Word. He promised "IT." And when she believes "IT" in her heart and speaks "IT" with her mouth, "IT" shall be done for her by her Father in Heaven. Others may choose to live a life dictated by the world's ever changing fads and latest prescriptions for happiness, but she is anchored to answers that are eternal. They produce real results. *"The grass withers, the flower fades, but the word of our God stands forever"* (Isa. 40:8 NKJV). God's Word is forever settled, so she can bank her entire life on "IT." She can give her life to "IT," and "IT" will build a new life for her.

The One who created her knows her. He has a plan for her life and can make all things new. With one simple prayer, one cry for help, He comes to the rescue, bringing "IT" with Him. When she gets Him, SHE GETS "IT."

how to have "IT"

To have "IT" you must first know the One who purchased "IT." To know Him, you need to speak to the Father and give Him your permission to "move in." He will not force Himself into your life, but will gladly take all of your brokenness and give you something beautiful instead—Himself. *"Everyone who calls on the name of the Lord will be saved"* (Acts 2:21). Then, as the Scripture says, *"I am my beloved's, and my beloved is mine"* (Song of Sol. 6:3 NKJV). You will never be alone again.

If you want "IT" and are not sure what to say to Him, I suggest something like this:

Father, I need You.

I want to be the woman who has "IT."

I have tried many other ways to make my life whole, but it won't work without You.

You created me, and only You know who I was created to be and how to give me the love, acceptance, and forgiveness I seek.

I surrender myself to Your love.

I accept the sacrifice of Jesus Christ, Your Son, for all of the shortcomings in my life, and I give myself to You.

I thank You that the old me has passed away, and everything in me is now new.

Do with me as You will. I am Yours. I know Your plans for me are good.

Thank You for making me a woman who truly has "IT."

And thank You that my eternal home is with You.

Amen! (Let it be so!)

After you have prayed for Jesus to take your life, then you have been "born again" into God's Kingdom. This is a new Kingdom with new ways and promises. Another promise that you can now receive is the gift of the Holy Spirit. The Bible promises to send you the Comforter, the Holy Spirit, to guide you and teach you all of God's truth. It won't all happen overnight, but He will do spiritual heart surgery on you as He did on me. You will experience a newfound love, peace, and joy. You will also have the power to be His follower. The Holy Spirit will help you have the ability to be the woman who not only has "IT," but also knows how to possess or own it. He will teach you and give you course corrections along the journey to your destiny.

The disciples asked a group of new converts in the Book of Acts, *"'Did you receive the Holy Spirit when you believed?' They answered, 'No, we have not even heard that there is a Holy Spirit'"* (Acts 19:2). Once they knew about this gift, they prayed and received an outpouring or baptism of the Holy Spirit. As they did, they began to pray in a language from Heaven. This new language caused them to be strengthened as they prayed using it. God's Spirit could speak new thoughts to them and give them a power from out of this world!

I strongly encourage you to ask Jesus to baptize you with the Holy Spirit as He promised in His Word and did for the believers in the Bible. Jesus said, *"Ask and you will receive"* (John 16:24). May I suggest this prayer:

> *Jesus, since You are in charge of my life now, I ask You to give me the promise You made to fill me with the Holy Spirit.*
> *I receive the Holy Spirit now. Thank You, Jesus.*

I thank You that the gifts of the Holy Spirit are now working in my life.

I have the power to live my life for You, and my life will become an example of Your love.

I can pray in a heavenly language and know that You will give me the revealed truth of God's Word. As I do so, I can live the abundant life You paid for me to possess.

I thank You I can also grow in the fruit of following after the Holy Spirit.

Thank You for filling me with the Holy Spirit.

I encourage you to pause and just wait on the Holy Spirit to begin to pray with you and speak through your voice and into your spirit.

If you prayed either of these prayers, I really want to know! I would love to hear from you, pray for you, and send you a free gift to help you continue in this amazing journey in Christ. Please write, email, or call me at:

Drenda Keesee
P.O. Box 779
New Albany, OH 43054
1-888-391-LIFE or contact me at www.drenda.com

call to Action

Everywhere I travel, I have women, especially younger women, approach me in tears and share how they do not have a mother figure in their lives. Many of them are from divorced families and at some point there was a disconnect with their mother. One beautiful young woman told me that her mother left her and her father when she was only ten, and she had to go through all the changes of adolescence and womanhood alone, with only her father to help her. Another young woman lost her mother to cancer and had to try to navigate through life and motherhood alone. One woman was abandoned by both her father and mother. There are many injustices and difficulties for these women to face, but there is also tremendous hope in God and His plan. In spite of their pain, all of these young women are flourishing because they have His love. He can truly comfort all who mourn, and bring beauty for ashes, the oil of joy for mourning, and the garment of praise for the spirit of heaviness (see Isa. 61:3).

Many years ago, a Ugandan minister prophesied that God was calling me to be a mother of nations and that I would share with women how to be a mother. I knew I had always felt a heavy burden for the struggles and pain of women and wanted to see them healed and whole, but I said in my heart, "God, how could You use me, and why would You use me? Remember, I'm the girl who was never going to marry or be a mother! And now You want me to be a mother to nations? I'm not sure You want me to do that."

But isn't that just like God. Just when we think we have a plan,

He always has a better one. And just when we think there is no hope for us, because we have made too many mistakes, *"Then God."* He steps in and turns our weaknesses into strengths, and the very area that once was our stumbling block becomes our soapbox! He delights in using the foolish things to confound the wise. I do not consider myself wise, but just wise enough to realize that apart from Him, I can do nothing. I don't want to be apart from Him, ever.

If you read Judges 4, you know that Deborah was a righteous woman who spoke truth in a time when great evil had tried to destroy her nation. Deborah was called a "mother in Israel" (see Judg. 5:7), and even when men were afraid to stand up against the enemy, she declared God's victory and plan in the face of negative circumstances and brought victory to her people. I believe God is calling us as women to be Deborahs in this hour— to be mothers: to nurture and impart the beautiful tender spirit of motherhood; to want more for our children (natural and spiritual children) than we have had; to do all we can to shield them from becoming brokenhearted. A mother emblazoned with the Spirit of God always wants more for her children than she has experienced herself. And there is nothing that can keep her from her child in need. I believe that kind of anointing of God's presence is on your life to make a difference.

Will you join me in a quest to use our influence as women, not to control or manipulate, but to give and release the spirit of motherhood into the earth through the Spirit of Jesus Christ? There are women all over the world who need to GET IT!

ABOUT DRENDA KEESEE

DRENDA KEESEE is cofounder of the international outreach Faith Life Now and, along with her husband, Gary, has been in the ministry for 15 years. Married for 28 years and the mother of five beautiful children, she is also an entrepreneur, author, speaker, and the co-pastor of Faith Life Church. Drenda has a heart and passion to help women see past the misconceptions and downright lies about how to be a happy woman, an excellent wife, mother, daughter, and lover of God. She shares from firsthand experience, using true stories, humor, and her contagious zeal to effectively communicate her faith. Her mission is to launch a movement to mobilize women to change their society, generation, and nation.

IN THE RIGHT HANDS, THIS BOOK WILL CHANGE LIVES!

Most of the people who need this message will not be looking for this book. To change their lives, you need to put a copy of this book in their hands.

> *But others (seeds) fell into good ground, and brought forth fruit, some a hundred-fold, some sixty-fold, some thirty-fold* (Matthew 13:8).

Our ministry is constantly seeking methods to find the good ground, the people who need this anointed message to change their lives. Will you help us reach these people?

> *Remember this—a farmer who plants only a few seeds will get a small crop. But the one who plants generously will get a generous crop* (2 Corinthians 9:6).

EXTEND THIS MINISTRY BY SOWING
3 BOOKS, 5 BOOKS, 10 BOOKS, OR MORE TODAY,
AND BECOME A LIFE CHANGER!

Thank you,

Don Nori Sr., Publisher
Destiny Image
Since 1982